The Dentist Guide to Creating Personal and Financial Freedom

2025 Edition Fully Revised and Updated

The Dentist Guide to Creating Personal and Financial Freedom

2025 Edition Fully Revised and Updated

DR. ALBERT "ACE" GOERIG

The Dentist Guide to Creating
Personal and Financial Freedom

by Dr. Albert "Ace" Goerig

ISBNs:
979-8-9913173-0-6 (softcover)
979-8-9913173-1-3 (eBook)

Published by

Doctor Ace LLC

222 Lilly Rd. NE

Olympia, WA 98506

DoctorAce.com

Table of Contents

Go to www.doctorace.com/to quickly access links to all the online resources that are referenced in this book.

ABOUT THE AUTHOR . . . ix

PREFACE . . . xi

FOREWORD . . . xiii

CHAPTER 1: CREATING A BEAUTIFUL STORY . . . 1

How to Bring Abundance into Your Life . . . 2

My Ninety-Year-Old Millennial Story: Creating a Lifestyle Practice . . . 3

A Tale of Two Dentists . . . 5

You Can Become a Multi-Millionaire. . . . 7

Writing Your Own Story . . . 7

CHAPTER 2: BECOMING MORE PROFITABLE IN YOUR PRACTICE . . . 9

Successful Practice Models . . . 12

Creating an Office Culture. . . . 14

Creating an Efficient Office . . . 15

Ideas and Systems That Can Double Your Net Profit . . . 16

Become a Stronger Leader . . . 27

Small Practice Changes Result in Enormous Increases in Net Profit 28
Raise Your Fees Annually 29
Hire a Practice-Management Consultant 30
What Do You Look for in a Practice-Management Consultant? . . 33
Use a Consultant to Help You Create a "Lifestyle Practice" . . 34

CHAPTER 3: GETTING OUT OF DEBT QUICKLY 37
Freedom Facts 37
Why We Pay Off Debt First 40
How to Make a 1,000% Guaranteed Investment Return . . . 43
Debt Is the Devil 45
Creating a Debt-Free Office 45
Lisa's Story 46
Eliminate All Debt in Three to Six Years 47

CHAPTER 4: ACHIEVING FINANCIAL FREEDOM 49
The Cost of Advisers 52
Learn How to Invest Safely and Simply on Your Own 55
Why We Invest in the Stock Market 55
Stock Cycles 58
Retirement Accounts and Taxes 62
Tax Strategies to Help You Reduce or Eliminate All Taxes on Your Investments 65
The 5 Common Mistakes You Need to Avoid While Planning for Retirement 68
Should You Buy or Rent a Home? 69
Estate-Planning and Asset-Protection Checklist 72
Financial Myths 74
Avoiding Financial Mistakes 78
Final Thoughts on Investing 82

CHAPTER 5: ENJOY LIFE, LIBERTY AND THE PURSUIT OF HAPPINESS 85
Enjoying Good Health 85
Creating Great Relationships 86
Learning and Understanding Meditation 88
Creating Love in Your Life 88
Letting Go of Issues and Emotional Pain from Your Past . . . 88
You Need to Take Care of Yourself First 89
Teaching Your Children About Loving Life and Finances . . 90
Stop Complaining 90
Let Go of All Anger 91
How Much Is Enough? 92
Get Rid of the Junk in Your Life 92
Don't Go Down the Rabbit Hole 93
Charitable Giving 93
The $2 Freedom and Happiness Bill 93
Learn to Love Your Life Now 96

FINAL THOUGHTS 99

APPENDIX A: STEP-BY-STEP DEBT-REDUCTION PLAN 101

DEBT-ELIMINATION WORKSHEET 109

MANAGING BUMPS IN THE ROAD 117

APPENDIX B: IDEAS ON HOW TO FIND AND MAKE MORE MONEY 119

APPENDIX C: LEARNING TO INVEST ON YOUR OWN 123
Rule One Investing 123
How to Start 126
Understanding Rule One Investing 129
Finding Wonderful Companies 132
Use the Four M's 132

Determine the Company's Intrinsic Value 133
Research Sources and Websites 138
Paper Trading 140
Thinkorswim Indicators, FACs and Trend Lines 141
The Floors and Ceilings 145
Understanding Dividends 148
Dividend Example 154
When to Sell 157
Where to Put Your Money Now 159
Should You Invest in Stocks or in Real Estate 161
The Pros of Investing in Stocks 162
The Cons of Stock Investing 163

PRAISE FOR *THE DENTIST GUIDE TO CREATING PERSONAL AND FINANCIAL FREEDOM* 165

About the Author

DR. ALBERT "ACE" GOERIG graduated from Case Western Reserve University Dental School in 1971 and was their distinguished alumnus in 2014. He retired from the Army Dental Corps in 1991 and has been in private practice for 34 years in Olympia, Washington. He has presented at every major national dental meeting and co-founded Endo Mastery, a coaching program for endodontists in 1996. He continues to see patients one day a week in a fun and effortless practice.

In 2004, he wrote his first book: *Time and Money: Your Guide to Personal and Financial Freedom*. His newest books are entitled: *The How-To Book on Dividend-Growth Investing—Create Generational Wealth and Passive Income for Life!* published in March 2023; *The Big Little Book on Creating Personal and Financial Freedom* in June 2024; and *The Secrets to Maximizing Dividend Stocks Returns* in October 2024. He has a free website, www.doctorace.com, with videos to help individuals quickly become debt-free and understand simple and safe investing. Dr. Goerig and his wife, Nancy, have been married for more than 55 years and have 5 children and 14 grandchildren.

Preface

AS DENTISTS, WE HAVE ONE OF the greatest professions, and, as Americans, we live in one of the greatest countries in the world, with all the opportunities to have the life of our dreams. Yet many dentists have yet to find happiness and contentment in their practice and their lives. One problem is that we were not taught in dental school the secrets of creating a great, fun and profitable practice. We have little education or understanding about personal finance and investing.

We are taught an old-age idea of retirement, where we work 30 to 40 years and hope we have saved up enough money to live well in retirement. This is what I call a life-sentence practice. What I want to introduce you to in this book is what I call a lifestyle practice. This is where we create a very profitable and fun practice, where we can eventually work only three days a week and have eight to 10 weeks off a year. During this time, we learn to invest on our own, creating a never-ending source of passive income.

Everything we have been taught about money is designed to keep us poor and others wealthy. We are taught to use financial advisors, who can take up to 70% of your investment return. Many dentists lose money by placing it into several various so-called investments that they know nothing about, such as annuities, risky stocks and speculative real estate, hedge funds, commodities, day trading and limited partnerships, hoping they will strike it rich.

We forget that the real money is made in our practice, and the best investment we can make is in ourselves. First, learn how to create a very profitable fun and successful practice. This is best done with a good practice-management coach. Next, focus all extra money on paying off all debts. As you pay off your debts, learn how to invest on your own safely and simply. This book will help you through that process.

We need to learn to love what we do and focus on creating a practice that is fun and profitable. My mentor, Kendrick Mercer, taught me that "Life is a process, not an end; if you don't enjoy the process, you'll hate the end!" This book is about learning to enjoy the process.

The message is simple: first, learn how to increase your practice profitability, pay off debts quickly and learn how to safely invest on your own, while maximizing your personal investment in a tax-free environment such as Roth IRA. This book will show you the path. Each of you has the potential of becoming debt-free in 3 to 7 years and financially free in 10 to 20 years. More importantly, you will enjoy your practice more while creating an incredible relationship with your patients, team and family. The rewards are many. But most of all, I urge you to enjoy the process.

Dr. Albert C. (Ace) Goerig
Olympia, Washington
January 2025

Foreword

YOU ARE ABOUT TO MAKE THE MOST important decision of your life. This process will begin when you realize that your past does not define your future. You have the power to write a new personal and financial story. This journey begins when you delve into Ace Goerig's secrets for creating personal and financial freedom for dentists.

I have known Ace for decades as a friend. I've also followed his career as a super-successful endodontist and one of the best coaches I know. His newest book has the power to become the guide through the financial minefields of myths and mistakes where dentists find themselves during their careers. Make no mistake: waiting until you are in your 50s or later is exactly the wrong strategy for a safe, secure financial future. All of us should strive for a future with a variety of choices and options in our lives, which we can secure by the actions and decisions we make today. The scary part of this realization is that most doctors don't realize their mistakes until it is too late. When it comes to eliminating debt and saving money, starting as soon as possible is fundamental. As with most things in life, there is never going to be perfect timing or a perfect situation. The secret is just starting where you are, now. I have had the honor to speak to thousands of dentists every year, and the one thing that I find they share is a lack of understanding of the basics of debt and financial freedom. This misunderstanding or lack of knowledge is the fundamental element in every doctor's struggles. Learn to control consumption debt, and you'll set into motion a lifetime of predictable wealth building.

For most of us, the struggle begins with the misunderstanding that debt is normal and unavoidable. Generations of people have assumed that they will always be in debt and that it is OK. But nothing could be further from the truth. Ace will give you real-life examples of his team members and friends who have bucked the trend and decided to re-write their stories. He has created a guide that has been found "tried and true" thousands of times. You are fortunate that you don't have to reinvent the wheel or spend one more day struggling, only to find another strategy that does not work. Ace outlines a concise, consistent financial plan for dentists, a playbook for success in life that works.

Michael Abernathy, DDS
National speaker and founder of Summit Practice Solutions
Celina, Texas

Chapter 1

Creating a Beautiful Story

IN A MAY 2017 INTERVIEW with Charlie Rose, Warren Buffett was asked what gave him his greatest joy. "I love going to the office," said Buffett. *"It has been my painting for more than 50 years: I get to paint what I want, and I own the brush, and I own the canvas, and the canvas is unlimited. And that is a pretty nice game, and I get to do it every day with people I like. I don't have to associate with anyone that causes my stomach to turn. If I were in politics, I'd have to smile at a lot of people I want to hit. I've got a really good deal, and I am hanging onto it."*

Most dentist-owners forget that they have the brush and the canvas, and the canvas is unlimited. They can create their story any way they want. Sometimes it takes frustration with the office, not enough time with family or getting into a rut before they start looking for another answer. They may need the insight of an outside source such as a coach to help them through the process.

We are here on this planet for a relatively brief period, and all we have is from now until the end of our lives. So, how can we make the most of this time? To live our lives to the fullest, we need to create a new vision or story of what is possible. We all can live the rest of our lives as a very exciting adventure. For most of us, because of the lack of business and financial training, it is difficult to set up a plan for reaching financial freedom.

After I retired from the Army Dental Corps, I opened a small dental practice. Without any understanding about how to run a practice, I became highly stressed and exhausted within the first six months and wondered if I had made the right decision. Realizing I needed help, I brought in Linda Miles, one of the best practice-management consultants in the country, and that made all the difference. She helped me create efficient office systems that allowed me to bring back the fun and profitability into my practice. Over the years I have hired multiple practice consultants; all have helped me grow, become more successful and create a practice I love.

In this book I want to share with you what I have learned from these practice-management experts. Each of you has the ability to create an incredible practice that is extremely profitable and allows you time for yourself and your family. Gandhi was once asked, "What is your message to the world?" He replied, "My life is my message." What is your message to your family and children?

HOW TO BRING ABUNDANCE INTO YOUR LIFE

The reason we create positive stories is to let the universe know what we want. I personally believe that we can bring anything—positive or negative—into our lives, depending on our thoughts. This happens by creating a clear, positive vision of exactly what we want and know (believe) that it will come about. This could be an increase in new monthly patients, doing more profitable treatments or finding the right associate or team member. Over 100 years ago, in his book, *The Science of Getting Rich*, Wallace Wattles talked about focusing on what you want and not what you don't want in your life. We need to put our energies into the creative and not the competitive aspects of life.

I believe in the success of all dentists and not in competition. There is unlimited abundance, if we have the right focus and vision, we can bring whatever we want into our lives. The real fun is helping others create abundance in their lives. I spend little time listening to the negative events in the news, which I cannot control. The real joy and happiness comes from taking incredible care of our patients and having a wonderful dental team. Abundance always comes when we are thankful for all the gifts and richness that we have in our lives.

MY NINETY-YEAR-OLD MILLENNIAL STORY: CREATING A LIFESTYLE PRACTICE

As members of the Baby Boomer generation, most of us were taught to work hard, put in the hours, take three weeks' vacation a year, and retire after 40 years of practice to play golf and enjoy the sunsets. Yet many dentists still work after age 65, not because they want to, but because they have to, due to poor management of their practice and their money, or because they have had too many "successful" marriages.

Baby Boomers sometimes look down upon Millennials because they seem to be more interested in enjoying life now, taking more time for themselves and their families, and are not as concerned with money as were Baby Boomers. Yet down deep, those two generations are more alike than they think. Because of our cultural imprinting, most Boomers did not know that we could write a better story. Let me tell you about my ninety-year-old Millennial.

When I first came to Olympia, Washington, one of my favorite referring dentists came in for a root canal. He was in his 70s yet looked like he was in his 40s. I commented on how great he looked, and I asked him what his secret was. He told me he'd created a lifestyle practice 10 years out of dental school.

In the mid-1950s, when he had graduated, most dentists worked 5 days a week and took about 2 weeks' vacation a year. After a year in practice, a classmate told him that he could really work 4 days a week if he just modified his schedule and make just as much money while having more time off. He did, and it worked. He told me he and his wife were not big spenders, so they were able to pay off his school loans, the mortgage on their house, the practice and all debt within 10 years of graduation.

Now he realized he needed to work only 3 days a week. He started taking more vacations each year to be with his family and enjoy his hobbies. He had more time for continuing-education courses and to be much more creative in the way he ran the practice. He paid his team on salary for four days a week, so they also had time off while funding their retirement plan. He eventually retired at age 82 and enjoyed his very long and loving marriage.

He came by my office in his early 90s and showed me pictures of himself skiing on the top of Mount Rainier with his great-grandson and fly-fishing with his daughter. He recently passed away, shortly after his wife died. He was one of my great mentors who taught me the importance of getting out of debt early and creating a lifestyle practice. He learned to invest on his own and created an ever-increasing passive income while living a full, fun and meaningful life. I am sure he enjoyed his Millennial-style life.

What most of us do not realize is that **we, too, can enjoy a lifestyle practice instead of a life-sentence practice.** We just need to create it, and, in dentistry, we can. We can do this by quickly getting out of debt while we create a practice that we love that is profitable and fun. Benjamin Franklin retired from business at age 46 to have more time to work on other interests and to contribute to the well-being of society while creating a personal legacy. What will be your legacy?

Don't do stupid things with money. The main mistake dentists make is living beyond their means right out of school and burying themselves in debt. Instead, know that you will have plenty of money to get out of debt quickly. As you become debt-free, learn how to invest consistently and safely on your own. To do this, you will need the right teachers, who I will introduce you to later in the book.

Everything you have been taught about money will keep you poor and make others rich. This is called the Great American Scam. It consists of monthly debt payments and has changed the American dream into a nightmare. We are lulled into a false sense of security and ownership. The banks have trained (fooled) us to stay in debt our whole lives through credit cards, mortgages, refinancing, and other loans, while they take from us two-thirds of our life's earnings in monthly debt payments. Unfortunately, most dentists do not understand how our money system really works.

A TALE OF TWO DENTISTS

Let's compare the tales of two 25-year-old dentists.

Dentist A earns $230,000 a year. He has fallen for the scam and lives big. He buys the big practice, big home, expensive cars, and other toys to build ego and to find happiness while continually creating more debt and making monthly payments. He has no savings or money for a practice consultant.

After 30 years, he has paid off his mortgage, practice, and school loan, but at age 55, he still has a second mortgage, car payments, credit cards, timeshare payments, and other debts, and only $225,000 in savings. He resents going to work because he is working to pay off debt and not for the relationships or the fun of it. This creates poor relationships with his family, patients and team.

He will give to his creditors two-thirds of his life's earnings, including the taxes he has paid on that income. Along with that, he will have given up his freedom and a life of choice, which will keep him working for many more years because he has to—not because he wants to.

Dentist B also earns $230,000 a year. However, Dentist B lives simply, like a student, and she learns how to be more profitable in dentistry, allowing her to pay off all debts, including credit cards, car, mortgage, school loans, and practice debt in 10 years. Within the first year of practice, she brought in a practice-management consultant, who helped her increase her net profit to $450,000 a year. Over the next few years, she will increase her yearly net to more than $800,000.

At age 35, she has no debt, has a lifestyle practice, and now works because she wants to, not because she has to. She loves going to the office three days a week, with 8 to 12 weeks off a year for vacation to be with her family and friends. She now has 60% to 70% of this income available to invest for retirement, children's education, travel or charitable contributions.

She has an associate, and the office is open 5 days a week. No one in the office works more than 4 days a week. Even though she works only 120 days a year, she will earn 4 times more than Dentist A, except she will go to the office for relationships and fun, not because she needs the money. She now has the time to enjoy her family, expand her relationships and other pursuits, including making a difference in her community and the world. At age 55, she will have been debt-free for 20 years. Because of her increase in net profit and understanding how to invest successfully in the stock market on her own, she now has a net worth of more than $15,000,000 while receiving $400,000 a year in ever-increasing passive income from dividend-producing companies.

YOU CAN BECOME A MULTI-MILLIONAIRE

Here are the lessons from the book *The Millionaire Next Door*, by Thomas Stanley and William Danko. Wealth is not the same as your income. Wealth is what you accumulate (net worth) and not what you spend. Wealth comes from working smart, dedication, planning and self-discipline. Millionaires do not live in upscale neighborhoods or drive fancy cars. A millionaire's goal is to become financially independent, which is much more important than displaying high social status. These financially successful people control their consumption and do not allocate too much money to products and services.

Millionaires are frugal and live well below their means. Most millionaires live in an average home and drive an older car; their their children go to public schools. They are married to the same spouse, who is also a conservative spender. Warren Buffett, one of the richest men in the world, has lived in the same modest house for more than 60 years, sent his children to public schools, and drives an 8-year-old car.

We all have choices about where we want to spend our money. Initially we could buy a smaller house, go on fewer vacations, buy a smaller car, or put more money into investments. Once we are debt-free, we can make the choices that add meaning to our lives. Most people do not consciously sit down and consider their choices, but, instead, they haphazardly spend their money without focus. Until we are debt-free, we are restrained by our income, so we need to create a game plan and focus our excess money to draw a guide of personal and financial success.

WRITING YOUR OWN STORY

The dentists I have coached over the years want to have more time off to enjoy their family, hobbies and personal time.

Initially, they are burdened by long-term debt, stressed at work, and exhausted when they come home. They are unable to see the possibilities that life and their profession have to offer.

Before you can create the life you want, you must first imagine it. With the right vision, game plan and coaching you could be debt-free within 3 to 7 years, work 3 or 4 days a week in a drama-free, stress-free office with the people you like. Once debt-free, you could take 6 to 10 weeks' vacation a year and have plenty of time to be with and create incredible relationships with your family.

So, whether you are a practice owner or an associate, you have the canvas, and you have the brush to create the life of your dreams. This book was created for you, to show you the possibilities in your practice and personal life and give you the tools, ideas and game plan to create your story. As you go through the book, write down the things you want to change in your life and the steps that you will take to create your new life story. The possibilities are endless.

Chapter 2

Becoming More Profitable in Your Practice

YOUR PRACTICE IS YOUR ECONOMIC ENGINE, so optimize it to the fullest. You can make more money in your practice by creating efficient systems, providing top-notch customer service, having a loving and incredible team, high efficiency, and beautiful clinical results.

In 1991, I retired after serving 20 years in the US Army and moved to Olympia, which needed an endodontist. A little afraid of opening my practice, I started in a small, three-operatory, 600-square-foot office that another dentist had just left. At that time, I knew very little about opening a private practice and had no practice-management experience, so I brought in a local dental consultant to help me set up my systems. She was very helpful, and we implemented systems and hired three assistants and one office administrator.

Being one of only three endodontists for a population area of 200,000, I was swamped with patients, and I was working 5 days a week, 10- to 12-hour days, killing myself and my team. I did not understand the business of dentistry or how to schedule patients properly. This resulted in excessive stress and very low production.

After six months, I was exhausted and wondered if I should have just retired from dentistry completely. There were a lot of complaints and drama from my overworked team. Some days I would drive up to the office and think that I should maybe just keep on driving. One Sunday, I came into the office and was going through the front-desk drawers and noticed a lot of bills that had not been paid and checks that had not been deposited. It turned out that the woman up front was overwhelmed with her duties but had not told me.

Eventually, I realized I was five months behind in payroll taxes, my life insurance had been canceled, and I had $250,000 in accounts receivable over 120 days. This is when the average dental practice was collecting $500,000 a year. I did not know we needed to collect at the time of service, and she did not have the time to send out statements. We were basically living on insurance payments.

Because I had lectured nationally on endodontics, I knew most of the great practice-management coaches on the circuit, and the best coach I knew was Linda Miles. I hired her to come in and turn my practice around. She was incredible and taught me the importance of efficient systems, keeping track of the important numbers, scheduling, marketing, and creating a superior team. We hired new employees and an experienced administrative-team member. I reduced the number of patients I saw, focused on enjoying each individual patient and the dentistry, and even got home on time. Within a month, I was working less, more profitable, and doing procedures I loved.

I also learned how to use practice monitors and know the numbers I needed to track, including understanding my profit and loss (P&L) statement. I hired a local bookkeeper to teach me how to use QuickBooks. I did my own QuickBooks for six months to better understand my overhead expenses and learn the ins and outs of QuickBooks. The same bookkeeper came to my home office twice a month and entered all of my personal and business numbers from my checkbook and credit-card statements into QuickBooks.

He also balances my checkbook and printed out all checks, including refunds. Each quarter he does my 941 federal tax return, state unemployment and state disability taxes, and city taxes. I also had him set up QuickBooks' $500-a-year payroll accounting program. This saved me from working with a payroll service at $2500 a year, and it was much easier for my office manager to put in payroll hours. I pay my bookkeeper $42 an hour and last year paid him $1,900 for my business and $600 for my personal accounting. He has a great knowledge of taxes and works very closely with my CPA.

I have an excellent CPA who used to work with the IRS. She oversees everything, gives me advice, and does my tax returns for around $7,000 per year. She is very responsive, up to date and thorough; she understands the IRS and ensures that we follow all the rules.

I review the profit and loss statement and office-production monitors monthly. You need to have good practice monitors, which you can obtain from one of your fellow dentists or a practice-management consultant. When you understand and monitor the numbers, there is less chance of embezzlement (staff-initiated bonus), an unfortunate but always real possibility. A two-doctor general-dentistry practice in my town was embezzled for $1.9 million over seven years, and it can happen to you if you don't know your numbers.

Since that time, I've had many different practice-management consultants come into my office, and every time, it has been of great value. I have been fortunate to be in one of the best dental communities in the country, where dentists are open to sharing and helping other new dentists in our community. Many of the ideas that I'm sharing with you come from my dental consultants, from the dentists in my local community, and from what I have observed in their practices.

The annual collections for the average general-dental office in the United States are around $770,000, with an overhead of around 69%, resulting in a net of $239,000 for the doctor. In this chapter you will find many strategies to increase profitability and reduce your time in the office. Below are four successful practice models of some of the best general practitioners I know.

In each of these real-life examples, the doctor has an empowered team to run the office, which allows the doctor to have 98% of her or his time to focus on direct patient care. Eighty-five percent of the success and profitability of the practice is dependent upon an empowered dental team and great clinical and management systems. The office has the right number of employees to reach high production goals. Each of these offices used a practice consultant to improve efficiency and double profitability. With increased profitability, it does not take a practice long to become debt-free, thus resulting in personal freedom and many more life choices.

SUCCESSFUL PRACTICE MODELS

Dr. K. Classic 2/2/2 model. This is a mature dental practice with two administrative team members, two dental assistants, and two hygienists. They all work four 8-hour days (32 hours) per week (185 days a year) with 6 weeks of vacation. The doctor is very efficient, highly skilled, and a great communicator with his patients. He focuses on high-quality restorative treatment and refers most of his periodontics, endo, and oral surgery out to local specialists, which further increases his efficiency. The team provides superior service to their patients and understands how to create an emotional connection with each patient. Dr. K collects $1.8 million per year with a 50% overhead, resulting in a $900,000 net profit. Remember that 80% of your production that is above your base overhead is net profit.

Dr. M. 2/3/2/1 model. This is an owner/doctor in her 40s with one associate. There are 2 administrative-team members, 3 dental assistants and 2 hygienists. The team works four eight-hour days (32 hours) per week. The owner/doctor works 3 days a week (125 days per year), and the associate works 2 days a week (90 days per year), compared to the average dentist, who works 195 days per year. The doctor is very efficient, highly skilled, and a great communicator with her patients. The practice has an excellent team that leads and manages the associate. They collect $2.9 million per year, with a 68% overhead, resulting in a $928,000 net profit for the owner/doctor. This is also a lifestyle-practice model.

Dr. H. 1/1/1 model. This model includes Dr. H., one administrative-team member, one assistant and one hygienist. They work four 9-hour days (36 hours) per week (180 days a year), with 6 weeks of vacation. The doctor is efficient and highly skilled; he communicates well with patients and has an excellent team. He collects $1.8 million per year, with a 50% overhead, resulting in a $900,000 net profit. He believes that the extra 4 hours per week (of which 80% is net profit) significantly increases his bottom line as compared to most offices that work only 32 hours.

Dr. N. (retired in practice) 1/1/1 model. Dr. N.'s practice includes one administrative-team member, one assistant, and one hygienist. They all work three 9-hour days (27 hours) per week (125 days a year), and all take 10 to 12 weeks of vacation. The team is paid a salary for a 32-hour week. The doctor is very skilled in dentistry and communication, and is efficient, with an excellent team. He collects $1,200,000 per year, with 50% overhead, resulting in a $600,000 net profit. He has been debt-free for years and has a strong base of patients who continually refer new patients to him.

Each of the above dentists quickly got out of debt and learned how to create passive income by investing on their own, using dividend-growth blue-chip stocks as described in this book. Each became financially free in their late 40s.

CREATING AN OFFICE CULTURE

The action of writing your vision is the most powerful way to make your new story happen. Once written and shared with the team, it becomes the culture of their practice. When writing about your new vision, think about the movie *Jerry McGuire,* and check out the YouTube video "Jerry McGuire Mission Statement."

Write a vision statement describing how you want your practice to be. This process will start you thinking about what is important to you in your practice as you create your office culture. A vision shows the world your intent to change and starts you on your new path. A vision makes a strong statement to the world about who you are and where you are going. It is like a magnet that will bring into your life all the ideas, people and tools you need to make it happen. It is also like a compass on a ship: it allows the captain to sail in a specific direction and helps guide the changes he needs to make to get to his new destination. Below is my own office vision statement, which I placed at the front office, where all patients can see it.

My Office Vision: *We are in a continual process of creating a story for our practice that is both fun and exciting and brings each of us personal fulfillment, joy, peace and freedom. Through dedicated people, ideas and the use of systems, we will develop a positive, nurturing and safe environment to grow and fulfill our needs both personally and professionally. It will be a place of mutual respect, laughter, clear communication and teamwork in an atmosphere that is fun, energized and joyous. We will connect with our patients on a personal level and provide* *a patient "Wow" experience that is so incredible that they will hesitate to leave our office for fear of entering a harsher world. Our office will have a reputation for high-quality treatment, being so gentle, safe and caring that we will receive many new referrals from our existing patients. We will enjoy every day to the fullest and live in each moment. Our office will be filled with laughter, pride, a sense of ease and a calmness that allows us to provide to each patient an experience that is unsurpassed.*

CREATING AN EFFICIENT OFFICE

Most dentists waste two to four hours a day on unproductive procedures that take too long and do not even pay attention to the overhead. Many spend too much time on a poorly designed schedule doing small-case, average procedures. Too much time is lost on the phone or computer, on team-management issues, or just talking too much. Many doctors think that improving their techniques or getting new equipment will increase their net profit, but 85% of real profitability is in efficient office systems and training the team to run those systems.

Dentists must learn to do the dentistry they enjoy and empower the team to manage the practice. The doctor can stop spending extra hours on practice-management issues. If you empower your team to run your practice, you need only three to four hours per month for practice management. The doctor needs to know the office numbers to ensure that there are no staff-initiated bonuses, which is called embezzlement.

Many dentists try to coach themselves and go to practice-management seminars and then come back and try to train the team to change their systems. The problem is that they don't know which systems to change. That's why it is essential to have an on-site consultant observe office flow and the quality of the team members, and then evaluate which systems can be improved and which systems need to be changed. The dentist/owner needs to let go of any members of the team who cause unnecessary drama and frustration to the doctor and other team members. When the systems flow well, patients love being in the office, the team loves serving the patients, and the dentist loves doing the dentistry. This whole process can be a lot of fun for everyone.

IDEAS AND SYSTEMS THAT CAN DOUBLE YOUR NET PROFIT

- **Phone and scheduling skills.** Today, most dentists feel they just don't have enough patient flow and believe they need to spend more time on external marketing. They could easily double their patient flow using effective phone skills with new patients. All-Star dental has an outstanding training program that ensures new patients come in for an appointment, but it also teaches your team superior customer service. All-Star Dental Academy. https://www.allstardentalacademy.com/

- **Presenting and selling dentistry.** You have the greatest case acceptance when you have a doctor, team and culture that can create an emotional connection with the patient. Because most dentists are uncomfortable presenting treatment plans and fees, this is best done through well-trained and incentivized hygienists.

- **Increasing internal referrals.** If you are not growing, you are not doing everything to inspire your patients to refer. Low-intensity referral is from 0 to 12 new patients per month. When you get below

10 new patients per month, it probably means you are offending them. When you get 13 to 25, that is normal; 26 to 40 is good, and above that is excellent. If you're getting 40 new patients a month and you are not growing, the problem is not consumerism, but capacity, which is space, equipment, team members and doctor's speed. It takes only one of these factors to be substandard to stop a practice from growing.

With high-intensity referral, of 25 to 40 new patients a month, patients are initiating the referrals. These are patients who call their friends just to tell them how incredible their dental visit was. When you obtain this level of referral intensity, you will draw patients from your entire area. Remember that 80% of your profitability comes from 20% of your patients. These are the patients who pay on time, appreciate you and your team, sing your praises, and have friends just like them. Focus your internal marketing on those patients.

How do you achieve true referral intensity? Patients love to find great value and share that with friends. If your patients get what they expect, then you're in the middle zone. If they get more than they expect, then you move to the highest level of referral intensity. Go through the office, and rate each step of the patient's experience as low, average or high. Any phone calls must be gracious and encouraging. When patients come to the office, they should be greeted by the person they talked with on the phone.

Referral negotiation is best facilitated by the team rather than by the doctor, and the following script must be delivered exactly (note that it is important to employ pauses long enough for the patient to focus on what you're saying).

Before treatment: Mrs. Jones, can I ask a favor? (Pause) If we can really impress you with how you're treated today, would you do something for us? (Pause; wait for the answer. Once they agree, continue.) If we can really impress you with how you're treated today, would you send us your friends, your family, and the people you work with? (Then wait for them to respond.)

After treatment: How did we do? Were you impressed? (When they say "yes," give them a couple of cards with some type of discount or offer printed on the back, so they can distribute them to their friends.) Creating an emotional connection with the patient begins with your first phone call with the patient, which is more about listening than talking. Each team member and the doctor need to be trained to ask more questions about the patient and talk less about themselves, so we listen and talk with the patient coming from our heart.

Sometimes, we get very fearful patients because of their poor past dental experiences. Before I meet the patient, my assistant tells me that the patient is very nervous, so when I come into the room and introduce myself, I tell them that I am very gentle. I will sit face-to-face with them and address their fears. I remind them that those fears from the past are embedded in their subconscious, so they have no control of the fear when they come into the office.

I also tell them that it takes great courage to face their fears and show up. Because of their courage, I promised them three things: I will always get them completely numb, they will always be in control, and

I am very fast and efficient in my treatment delivery. This helps put the patient immediately at ease. Creating that connection is where the fun is. More importantly is that, when you speak to a patient, you speak from your heart—not your head. This allows you to create an emotional connection with that patient. Here is a thank-you note from one of my patients that demonstrates the importance of emotional connection.

"Dear Dr. Goerig: Two weeks ago, I got a diagnosis of breast cancer stage IV. Two days after that I woke up with a swollen cheek and learned I needed a root canal and ended up in your chair. I was still emotionally reeling from my health news but noticed the poster from your time at Fort Knox, Kentucky. I was stationed there as an Army dietitian and, when I shared all my story, you were so gracious, compassionate and funny that you helped me relax and almost enjoy my time in your chair. Thank you for letting God use you to minister to me and reassure me of his love and care. You may not have been aware of it, but you were my angel that day! I still tear up thinking about it, how you verbally encouraged me, loved me, encouraged me further, and then even reduced my charges, so I would not be facing such a huge bill. You are an angel, and I can't thank you enough for being the conduit of God's love to me that day. I really needed it and won't ever forget it. God bless you and your whole family. With gratitude."

- **Same-day service.** There is another practice hidden within your practice. If you have a practice that schedules $75,000 per month, there is another $75,000 hiding in same-day service. The hygienist reminds patients of a condition that has already been diagnosed or just found and asks them if they would like to do the treatment that day. Case acceptance is far higher with same-day service. Once your office embraces the idea of same-day service as a normal part of doing treatment, handling the finances is not a problem. We only incentivize same-day service that is highly productive ($700 or higher) and that we want to do. The bonus for the person who gets a patient to say "yes" is $10, and the bonus for the assistant is $5. Same-day service is the secret to a high case average. When you try to sell harder on the first appointment, you can drive patients away from your practice. When the case average (total practice production divided by all new patients) rises above $2,500, referrals go down. When case average rises due to same-day service, referrals may rise at the same time. Low case average usually means high volume, which means more team members, more overhead and lower profitability.

- **Bonus system.** During my Army career, I would work very hard for three years in an assignment to get a 10-cent ribbon. This same incentive doesn't work as well in civilian life, but showing your appreciation through bonuses and thanking your team members often does pay big dividends. One of the most effective ways to increase profitability is to implement a smart and effective bonus system that can motivate your team while it increases your net profit.

  To make a bonus effective, everyone on the team must understand how the bonus is calculated. It is much better to give bonuses on a daily or monthly basis instead of yearly. That way, you get much more excitement and participation from the team. Bonuses should be designed to reward the entire team, not just individuals, although individuals can be rewarded for doing same-day service work or for increasing case acceptance.

All bonuses must be based on collections, with the understanding that total team compensation should not exceed 20%. Large purchases should not be added to average overhead expenses when considering this 20%. When you are trying to help your team get out of debt, remind them that bonuses can accelerate their debt reduction.

There are many types of bonus systems out there, and I would highly recommend that you work with a practice consultant who will help you implement a bonus structure that works best for you in your practice. I feel the best and most immediate bonus that you can give your team is to compliment them and thank them often for specific things, such as filling the schedule properly, creating great relationships with your patients, and making same-day service work. Individually, I thank each of my team players for being part of our incredible team.

- **Adult oral-sedation dentistry**: Fear of dentistry is one of the main reasons that only 65% of the population go to a dentist. Many of those with the greatest fears have extensive dental work that needs to be done. Becoming certified in adult oral sedation will help you take better care of your fearful patients, and it should be available for those patients who would like to have extensive work done all at one time under sedation.

The best course for dentists is provided by DOCS education. It is by far one of the best courses I have ever taken. They also have an IV-sedation certification course. https://www.docseducation.com 855-227-6505

- **Practice membership and becoming insurance independent.** Those who truly want a lifestyle practice have learned to drop most dental insurances. A practice-management consultant can help many practices drop their dental insurances and become fee for service. One way of doing this is to create practice membership. In this model, the patient pays a certain amount each year, such as $150 to $197 per person, which includes a 10% to 15% discount on all the dentistry during the membership year. For this membership, you provide an exam, X-rays and two cleanings per year (you can knock off $20 for children). You can offer to upgrade patients to this program once they need dental treatment. Membership patients are usually uninsured but can be offered discounts to encourage large treatment plans. Some states are trying to restrict practice-membership plans due to the pressures of dental-insurance companies. Check with your state.

- **Focus on the dentistry that is less stressful and more profitable.** Focus on and become extremely efficient on the 20% of the dentistry that gives you 80% of your profit. It always seems that the most profitable and successful dentists in town refer out a lot of their specialty work. The average profitable dentist in our area collects around $800,000 and takes home only $300,000 net. One of my best referrals learned from the prosthodontist how to do incredible, beautiful crown preparations in 5 to 10 minutes. This doctor collects about $1.5 million per year and takes home around $750,000 net. This is because he focuses on the procedures he does efficiently and less stressfully and refers out the rest. The reason for the high net is that 85% of the collections above $800,000 go to net profit.

- He once told me that the greatest enemies of the general dentist are difficult patients, stressful procedures, and unpredictability. That is why he refers most of his endodontics and other nonrestorative treatments out to specialists. I have personally found that the most profitable dentists in my community have strong professional relationships with the specialists.

- **Develop a win-win relationship with your specialist.** Specialists help you to be more profitable by allowing you to refer those cases that are stressful and not profitable and instead to focus on the dentistry you do best. They are a resource for you to expand your knowledge and can help and support you with difficulties in treatment. They are a second opinion and support your treatment plan. I also like to tell referred patients what a great office and dentist they are coming from during my treatments. Specialists also can be a source of referrals. And one thing that is often overlooked is that, the more we share, the more abundance comes into our lives.

- **How to improve speed and quality.** During the day, have your dental assistants time you. If you are taking too long on various procedures, such as molar root canals, get additional training or refer out to a specialist. Ask your local supply rep for the name of the best and most respected dentist in town, and ask the local lab owner which dentist does the most crown work with the highest quality. Call the doctor and ask if you can observe them in their office. You may want to video the procedure. Ask if you can bring your chief clinical assistant and front-office team member to observe the flow of the practice. Buy lunch for the doctor's team. Meet with the doctor for dinner and ask if he or she will mentor you. All great dentists are always looking for someone they can teach. Get involved in local study clubs.

- **Add new profitable services to your practice, and learn to master them.** Such services may include Invisalign or dental sleep medicine that focuses on the use of oral appliance therapy to treat sleep-disordered breathing, including snoring and obstructive sleep apnea (OSA).

- **Buy the patient records from another practice** when that dentist is retiring.

- **The office should be a place of safety and peace for the entire team**. Set free (fire) all employees who create drama in your practice. You cannot change people, but you can change (fire) people.

- **Handling clinical or office frustrations**. When things are not going exactly the way you want, don't get upset—just laugh. Or you can use the following words to refocus and stay on task: great, next, isn't that interesting, or it is what it is. Frustration and anger are detrimental to obtaining high-quality clinical results and creating a fun and profitable office.

- **Have an updated, superior website.** This is one of the first places a referred patient will go to check you out. It must have good photos, good information, and testimonials from your patients. It should be designed so that your website on your phone looks exactly like it does on the computer. It should have a patient-review area and a testimonial section. It is a good idea to have these testimonials moving across the page, so that, when a patient looks at their phone, they see the testimonials.

- **Addressing negative family and cultural imprints about success**. Many dentists do stupid things with money because they have no formal training in understanding financial matters. But the biggest issues are the imprints and cultural beliefs about money that we learned from our family.

  Some examples are, you have to work hard to earn money; getting rich is a matter of luck; money is the root of all evil; when things are going well, they will always go bad. You may have felt unworthy as a child, and this imprint prevents you from being successful and profitable in your practice, thus causing you to sabotage your own success in practice and your investments. One of the hardest things I need to do, as a coach, is to help clients get past their low deserve level that is embedded in their subconscious and prevents them from becoming more profitable and happier in their lives. This is also true when investing their money.

The purpose of this book is to provide a simplified investment game plan to learn how to invest on your own without the need of a financial adviser's risky investments, and other situations where you would lose your money. I knew one doctor who continued to self-sabotage in his investments and practice. He fortunately got a great dental coach, who helped him create a highly profitable practice, and he was finally able to put enough money away so he could retire. After he sold his practice and retired, he had all the money he needed to enjoy a fun and exciting retirement.

Unfortunately, his inner demons took over again, and he invested all his earnings from the practice into a real-estate deal where he lost it all. Those doctors who continually self-sabotage and do stupid things with money may find themselves living on their Social Security in their children's home and taking vacations in a 200-mile radius.

If you have poverty-consciousness imprinting or a low deserve level, you need to get professional help to break your behavioral patterns around money. One company that has helped many of my coaching clients is Legacy Life Consulting at https://www. legacylifeconsulting.com/. They will help you address the issues that cause you these problems and help you understand prosperity consciousness. With their help, you can create a story that allows you to expand your life and move out of your old comfort zone.

BECOME A STRONGER LEADER

The owner/doctor is the source of and is responsible for writing the vision based on his or her core values, which create the culture of the practice. Leaders must be authentic and trust in themselves, always learning and open to all possibilities, and willing to accept change. When you are not leading and paying attention, there will be much more drama in the team because they have lost respect for you. Great leaders empower their team to lead, but each senior team member knows the vision and direction of the practice is coming from the doctor.

Doctors will sometimes give up the leadership role because they're trying to be nice, and they do not like conflict. But when the doctor gives up the leadership role, someone will step in to take over that role. When you get clear and want to step back into the leadership role, you will get pushback from the person who has led the team, and they will resent you because it appears you did not appreciate their efforts. This may end up in the dismissal of that great employee. Great leaders win hearts before minds. Read Simon Sinek's book *Start with Why: How Great Leaders Inspire Everyone to Act*. Here are a few ways to keep growing as a leader:

- Give up control, delegate, and empower the team.
- Get out of the way, but follow up.
- Know the numbers (use practice monitors).
- Spend 98% of your time in direct patient care.
- Lead by example, and be the best employee.
- Tell the team what you want.

SMALL PRACTICE CHANGES RESULT IN ENORMOUS INCREASES IN NET PROFIT

It is amazing how an increase of just one more crown a day (by doing same-day service) can affect your net profitability. Look at the chart below. **One more crown per day increased the net profit by 181%,** from $197,647 to $357,647, resulting in a net annual income increase of $160,000. If you did two additional crowns per day, you would realize an extra $320,000 in increased net income. With this extra $320,000 per year, your entire school-loan debt, home and practice loan could be paid off in five to six years. Once you are debt-free, you will have three times the amount of money to be able to work less, invest, and enjoy your personal freedom. This is all possible if you are open to new ideas and dental coaching.

	One More Crown per day		**Average Dentists**	
	Amount	%	Amount	%
Collections	$802,583	100%	$602,583	100%
Overhead	$444,935	39%	$404,935	67.2%
Net profit	$357,648	61%	$197,647	32.8%
Daily collections	$4,013/day		$3,012/day	
Monthly collections	$66,881/month		$50,215/month	
4 days/week worked	200 days/year, with two weeks off			

The best dental practice-management book written is by Michael Abernathy, DDS, entitled: *The Super General Dental Practice: Everything Is About to Change*. You're about to discover how to transform into the practice you never thought possible. To get a free copy of the book, go to: https://summitpracticesolutions.com/the-super-general-practice/

Here are a few great websites for practice-management ideas. Each of these also offers practice-management coaching.

https://blatchford.com/
https://summitpracticesolutions.com/
https://www.whitehallmgt.com/
https://www.allstardentalacademy.com/

RAISE YOUR FEES ANNUALLY

Many dentists do not get around to raising their fees annually or semiannually. I recommend that you routinely raise your fees 2% to 4% a year just to keep up with inflation and the rising cost of dental materials. Even though you are locked in by some insurance plans, you should routinely do this for all other patients. Most owners do not understand the power of raising fees to increase net profit. If you have a $100,000 per-month practice and your overhead is 70%, your net profit would be $30,000 that month. A 10% increase in fees would give you an additional $10,000, and when added to your net of $30,000, you would have a total net of $40,000. This is a 33% increase in your profit.

Below is a chart that shows you how a 1%, 3% and 5% increase could affect the total net income of your practice over 30 years. Go to ADA.org/feesurvey to get a free 2025 fee guide for your area. These are free for ADA members.

You can also purchase the updated fee guide for your ZIP Code from Wasserman-medical.com for $169. Try to keep fees that the patients call about in the 80th percentile. Because of dental-insurance companies' pressures, you cannot collaborate to set fees with other dentists, but you can ask them what their fee guide is and then make your own decision regarding what your new fees will be. You may also hire someone to negotiate your fees with your insurance companies. (Check out Becky Balok at www.bbdentalconsulting.com.)

Increase Net Profit by Increasing Fees

Totals	Yearly Collections	Total Collections Increase		
		1% per year	3% per year	5% per year
30 years	$500,000	$2,556,370	$9,501,339	$19,880,395
30 years	$1 million	$5,112,740	$19,002,678	$39,760,790
30 years	$1.5 million	$7,669,110	$28,504,017	$59,641,185

HIRE A PRACTICE-MANAGEMENT CONSULTANT

Why spend the money to bring in a dental consultant? The answer is simple: To help the doctor and team reach their full potential, especially when what they are doing right now is not working. Doing more of it just becomes frustrating and exhausting. I think the big reason many dentists resist is that they are afraid to give up control of the practice or that it might not work.

Warren Buffett said the most important thing you can do is invest in yourself and your team. Many dentists have never taken the time to set up an efficient business model. 80% of practice success comes from having an empowered team that runs the practice and allows the dentist to do the quality dentistry that they know how to do. To significantly increase practice profitability, hire a coach who is familiar with your type of practice (that may include areas such as sleep apnea, conscious sedation, Cerec crowns, etc.) or who has a good track record of success. Just by modifying a few things in practice, dentists can often double their net profit.

Adding just one more crown per day could increase net profit by more than $300,000 a year. Having systems in place to schedule patients more efficiently, doing same-day service, collecting fees at the time of service, emphasizing more profitable procedures and raising fees are all examples of best practices that significantly increase the bottom line without raising overhead.

Most dental consultants can modify your business model so that you work three or four days a week instead of five and take four to eight weeks off each year for vacation. Profitability increases to a point where the doctor can pay off all debt within three to seven years. This is accomplished through systems and creating an incredible story: lifestyle practice. With this model, why would anyone ever want to retire?

Dentistry is changing rapidly, and many forces are causing stress. Some of the external forces over which we have no control are more corporate offices, increasing overhead due to insurance companies controlling fee growth, more general dentists and fewer dentists retiring; the big one one is the money spent on retail shopping, vacations and timeshares instead of maintenance dentistry. We need to learn to stop stressing over things we cannot control and focus on what we can control.

Things we can control are internal factors such as low production, doctor and team compensation, fewer patients, tougher cases, open schedules, no-shows, last-minute cancellations, student debt, office drama and overwhelming administrative challenges. If your practice is not growing, it is declining. More than 70% of all practices declined over the past few years.

Many dentists are frustrated and stressed in their practice. They think attending a practice-management course will help them clear these problems. The real problem is that they don't know what is wrong and what they can really fix. Many have already spent too many hours trying to control their practice. The most important service a practice-management coach can provide is to determine those issues that are holding you back and help you correct the systems and team issues that plague your practice. This is why the consultant must come to the office for a day to speak with the team and observe the office flow and schedule.

Most dental students pay more than $100,000 a year for their education, which does not include anything about practice management or efficient systems. Yet they balk at paying a consultant $50,000 to change the practice to make it more fun, less stressful and much more profitable. They see the consultant's fee as an expense and not an investment. Your practice is the economic engine of your life—it's where your money is made. Many dentist engines are broken and need to be repaired or tuned up. A good dental consultant can maximize the efficiency of that engine, resulting in two times or more increase in your net profit.

I have a different practice-management consultant come into my office every three to four years, and it has always resulted in increased profitability. Many of these companies will do a free objective analysis of your practice and help you understand where improvement is needed.

More importantly, the doctor who uses a consultant is finally creating a practice that she or he loves, with an A-team and happy, enthusiastic patients and high profitability. By implementing successful coaching, the doctors can increase their vacation time by an additional two to four weeks a year and still increase productivity. Remember that Uncle Sam pays 35% to 50% of the consulting fee in tax savings; if you have a partner, you also split the investment with him or her.

Most doctors pay off a consultant's fee in the first three to six months with increased collections. The two questions you must ask yourself after trying to change all the issues in your practice are, "How is what I am doing now working?" and "What is the true value of time with my family and time for myself?" Consulting helps you get peace of mind and your freedom.

When you're looking for a consultant, I would initially check with your dental colleagues and the most successful practices in your dental community who have used coaches. Ask them how good their experience was and, most importantly, what the result was from their coaching process. When selecting a consultant, it is important that you have a compatible philosophy of practice and that the consultant understands your needs and concerns.

Make sure any consultant you consider uses online monitors to help you understand and track your important numbers and monitor your progress. You must be clear about your own goals and believe that the consultant's philosophy will fit you and your team. So, give yourself permission to be your best, and to reach your and your team's full potential.

WHAT DO YOU LOOK FOR IN A PRACTICE-MANAGEMENT CONSULTANT?

- Has significant experience working in a dental office.
- Has significant experience working as a consultant.
- Can show you a track record of results.
- Can give you three to four references from dentists they have coached.
- Understands your problems and gives you insights and suggestions.
- Can help you become a better leader and help you give up control.
- Has an extremely positive personality, not negative or condescending, and can create a strong working and teaching relationship with your team and team leaders.

- Understands the numbers (and can teach you how to understand the numbers).

- Offers a program that is individualized to you and your practice, not cookie-cutter.

- Comes to your office, so that there is no loss in your production time.

Very few dentists see coaching as an investment that can give them a more-than 1000% return on that investment over time. Many dentists wait until they are tired, exhausted and have had enough pain. One famous quote was, "When the pain to remain the same exceeded the fear to change." If you are not ready or open to new systems, unable to let go of control and empower your team, unable to fire a bad employee, or think you already know the answers, then you are not ready for coaching. Working with a coach requires the willingness to implement positive change for both you and your team. If you can face your fears and are open to change, the rewards are many. The greatest reward is freedom in your personal and professional life. Transform your practice, and you transform your life.

USE A CONSULTANT TO HELP YOU CREATE A "LIFESTYLE PRACTICE"

In our culture, retirement has somewhat of a negative connottation, indicating old age, too old to work, or a reward for working hard for 40 years. I do not buy into this antiquated concept of retirement. By my definition, retirement is the time of many choices, opportunities and excitement. I believe you can begin your retirement when you're young through the concept of "lifestyle practice." This happens when you become debt-free, which allows you to have unlimited choices for your life, even in your thirties, forties and fifties.

There is an old phrase that says, "If you think you are what you do, then, when you don't, you aren't." We must stop thinking that we are just a dentist our whole life, because once we retire, who are we? A lifestyle practice allows us to have many experiences, careers and adventures, including dentistry. I don't think any dentist would like his tombstone to say, "He was a good dentist." This is about creating a legacy in your life that is much larger than one profession and makes a difference in your family, your community and in the world.

We all can choose to work one or two days less a week, thus allowing us to spend more time with our family when we are young. Another choice is to take more time off for travel, to teach, to create or enjoy your hobbies, or work on your bucket list. Ask yourself what message you send to your children about how to live life. Give them the example, throughout your life, of what real retirement (choices) looks like. A good consultant can show you how to increase your profitability, get out of debt early and work fewer days. They can also help you bring in an associate when the time is right.

Your practice can always be a constant source of income, and it can allow you to work as many days as you want. There may be a time when you are debt-free and financially free and would just like to work one or two days a week with associates. There is no right answer, but you do have choices and the time to figure out what works best for you. You and your spouse need to create this story together.

A lifestyle practice begins with a beautiful vision, the right systems, scheduling, great team, efficient techniques and marketing. Once you become totally debt-free, which happens much sooner when you have increased your practice profitability, you can bring in an associate who will help you increase your net profit. Hire doctors who want to be long-term associates and who do not want to have any of the issues involved with running a practice or ownership. They must be compatible with you and have the same treatment philosophy.

I am not a fan of dental partnerships because it complicates the decision-making process and reduces your profitability. Remember, in a 50/50 partnership, the spouse of your partner may end up controlling the decision-making for your entire practice. If you plan to sell your entire practice to the associate within a few years, then you can move into a partnership.

With an associate, you can now drop to three days a week, be open five days, and take much more vacation time because your practice is covered. You have the time to take more and better continuing-education courses to improve your skills. When you work fewer days, you are more refreshed, do higher-quality treatment, and enjoy your practice more. You create an empowered team that runs the practice, but you maintain complete control. Re-program your belief that you need to work hard. Be and live healthy while creating the adventure of your life.

Instead of selling your practice, another option is to bring in another associate and come into the office four hours per month, just to check in with the team and review the numbers. You can take home half of your previous net without doing dentistry.

To do this, you need an empowered team that runs the practice while providing an ideal patient experience through loyal associate doctors and motivated team members. To maximize the practice's success, work with a practice-management consultant each year to ensure that all systems are monitored, new team members are trained, and office leaders are supported to enable the doctor's goals to be met.

I am not a fan of multiple offices, as it takes much more energy and time for the owner/doctor to manage and handle all the problems associated with these offices. Create a great practice in one location, and focus on having great patients, a great team and time to enjoy your life.

Chapter 3

Getting Out of Debt Quickly

Freedom Facts

WHEN PUTTING ALL INVESTMENTS in perspective, the best returns are from paying off debt and increasing your practice profitability. These choices can give you a return of more than 100%. Below are the past 10 years' average returns on various investments.

- Home: 0–5%. According to Zillow, while home prices have appreciated nationally at an average annual rate between 3% and 5%, depending on the index used for the calculation, home-value appreciation in different metro areas can appreciate at markedly different rates than the national average. Over time, home values stagnated after factoring in inflation. Plan on spending 5% of the value of the home to buy it, 10% to sell it, and 1% to 2% a year to maintain it.

- Average actively managed fund investment: The average fund underperformed its benchmark by 1.75% per year before taxes and by 2.58% on an after-tax basis.

- Inflation: As of January 2025, the annual inflation rate in the United States was 3% for the 12 months ending in June. In 2022, we saw that rate increase up to 9%.

- Short-Term Bonds: As of January 2025, the one-month treasury rate is at 5.48%.

- S&P 500: The historical average yearly return of the S&P 500 is 10.64% over the last 100 years, as of end of January 2025. This assumes dividends are reinvested. Dividends account for about 40% of the total gain over this period. Adjusted for inflation, the 100-year average return (including dividends) is 7.214%.

- No-fee investing: Paying no fees on your investments results in getting you up to 70% more on your investments. Paying 1% to 4% in fees to financial advisers, brokers, or mutual-fund companies that actively manage your investments could cost you 70% of your return, making you work 10 to 15 years longer before you can retire. You need to learn how to safely invest on your own. This book will show you why.

- Routine practice-fee increases: These can produce a 10% to 30% increase in net profit every year.

- Paying off debt: Up to 1000% (10x) return.

- Dental practice-management consulting: Up to 1000% (10x) increase on return of investment over time.

Most of your advisers will not appreciate these numbers because they will not be able to make money from you. Also, each of them looks through a different lens, based on their experience and training. Each of them will have a different agenda for you and your money. Your banker's motivation is to get your money into their bank, so they can lend it back to you. Your CPA gets paid to do your state and federal income tax and keep you out of tax difficulty. Because most accountants do not understand business and are risk-averse, their advice would be not to do coaching because they cannot understand the benefits, and they see it as just an expense.

Surprisingly, some CPAs are concerned that an increase in your net income would increase your taxes—and they see that as a bad thing. Your investment adviser will encourage you to put your money into your investments and a 401(k) plan, so they can continue to receive fees. When it comes to your money, you are the only one who cares more about it than any of your advisers.

You will see how the power of paying off debt can give you a guaranteed return of 100% to more than 1000%, without risk or tax consequence. Many owner/dentists could double their net profit in one year by bringing in a competent practice-management consultant. This will magnify to more than 1000% in 10 years.

Everyone needs to focus on what investment of your time and money produces the greatest returns. If you execute the last four above strategies correctly, you will have more money than you will ever need, which you can trade in for time, freedom and choices. The stock market becomes a place to compound some of your excess money. I will show you the best strategies to safely get the best returns by yourself, without paying the extraordinarily high fees and commissions of financial advisers and brokers.

Once debt-free, a dentist would be able to maintain their lifestyle, fund their retirement, need to work only three days a week, still take off 8 to 12 weeks a year, and live a lifestyle practice. They could create a beautiful story and environment for themselves and their teams, and love going to the office knowing they have plenty of time off to play. Under those circumstances, why would you ever want to retire?

When this strategy is implemented correctly, you will have created an automatic investment program through high-dividend-producing companies, and you will not worry about the ups and downs of the market. Knowing that you are in for the long run and will not sell, eventually you can live off all the dividends of these companies. Remember that increasing the productivity of your practice and paying off all debt first, before investing in the market, will safely provide the highest returns without risk and with much more predictability.

WHY WE PAY OFF DEBT FIRST

The fastest way to become financially free is to pay off all debts before you put money anywhere else. The advantages to paying off debt first are:

1. Easiest and simplest to do and understand.
2. Can make more than 100% return on your money, guaranteed, without risk or taxes.
3. Can be done automatically, right out of your bank account.
4. Changes you from a spender into a saver.
5. Your paid-off home acts like a long-term inflation-adjusted bond. The 20% of your income that you

were using to pay off your mortgage now becomes a bond-like investment, getting 20% return on your paid-off home.

6. Once debt-free, you have three times the amount of disposable income (previously, two thirds of your disposable income was paid toward debt) to spend on investments and enjoying life.

One of the biggest misconceptions that keeps you in debt that is perpetuated by banks and accountants is that you should not pay off your house early, because when you have a mortgage, you can write off the interest rate on your taxes. This allows the banks to continue to get a large amount of interest from you using your money.

Let's look at this closely: in 2025 an average American couple who pays $10,000 a year in interest on their home loan has the choice of either taking the standard deduction of $29,200 or itemizing their return and taking the $10,000 tax write-off. When they itemize, they are unable to take the standard deduction of $29,200 and have an overall loss of $19,200 in standard deduction. The biggest loss is in the interest you paid the bank, which could range to more than 200%.

Pay attention—this is important: below is an example of a $310,000 mortgage at 4.5% for 30 years. You can see that, in the first year's loan payment of $18,849, only $5,001 goes to principal, but $13,848 goes to interest, which is lost forever to you. **This is a 277% loan, not a 4.5% loan.**

In the 28% tax bracket, you had to earn around $17,724 and pay taxes on that to get the $13,848 to give to the bank as interest payments, which makes it really a **354% loan**. If you had paid an additional principal payment of $5,231, you would have eliminated one year's payment, saved $13,618 in interest, and made 354% return on your money, guaranteed, without risk or any tax consequence.

Year	Interest	Principal	Balance
2025	$13,848	$5,001	$304,999
2026	$13,618	$5,231	$299,768
2027	$13,378	$5,471	$294,297
2028	$13,126	$5,722	$288,575
2029	$12,863	$5,985	$282,590
Total (after 5 years)	$68,833	$27,410	$282,590

The reality: over the next five years, you would have paid $96,243 in loan payments, and only $27,410 would have gone to pay off the loan. You must understand that the interest is always the highest at the beginning of the loan, and, for the first ten years of a 30-year loan, the interest paid will always be more than 100%. By paying off debt early, you can take advantage of this guaranteed high return. The bottom line: you invested $5001 and made $13,848, which is a guaranteed 277% return without risk. With this great return, why would anyone not use the money in their savings (only earning less than 1%) instead of paying off their home? You should also cash out any non-tax-deferred stocks and pay off debts.

When we have debt, saving money is an encoded trap that keeps us poor. In the above example, if we have $100,000 in your savings or non-tax-deferred investments, the best, safest and highest return on that money is to pay off debt. Paying that $100,000 toward the $310,000 home mortgage would drop your mortgage to $210,000 and **immediately save you $121,360 in interest payments while paying off 13 years of the mortgage. https://www.drcalculator.com/mortgage/old/**

You must see the $100,000 put into the house as a high-return, safe, long-term inflation-adjusted bond that is always available to you through lines of credit or second mortgages. Once the home is paid off, the money used for mortgage payments becomes a constant source of available cash flow. It is like getting money from a bond.

Remember, focus on paying off debt before you put your money anywhere else. While you are paying off debt, you can learn to invest in the stock market on your own—without risk—through paper trading as will be discussed below. Most people can be debt-free within five to ten years when they focus their money correctly. Below are two Excel charts that show exactly how much interest you are paying over a certain period of years.

HOW TO MAKE A 1,000% GUARANTEED INVESTMENT RETURN

Today interest rates for mortgages and dental-school loans can average anywhere from 6% to 8% per year. **Look at an actual 30-year, $300,000 dental-school or home loan with an interest rate of 7.9%, for which the doctor pays $2,180 per month. During the first year of repayment, only $2,556 goes to principal, and $23,608 goes to interest.** The doctor must earn around $30,000 and pay tax on those earnings, to cover that amount of interest each year. This is more than 1000% return on your investment. When determining how much student loan you will need, remember that, for every $1000 you borrow at 7.9% interest, initially, you may have to pay initially $10,000 in interest back to the bank, which does nothing to pay back the loan.

Year	Interest	Principal	Balance
2025	$23,609	$2,556	$297,444
2026	$23,399	$2,766	$294,678
2027	$23,173	$2,992	$291,686
2028	$22,928	$3,237	$288,449
2029	$22,662	$3,503	$284,946
Total (after 5 years)	$115,771	$15,054	$284,946

In this example, by making one additional principal payment of $2,766 that year, you will eliminate (save) $23,399 that you will never have to earn and give to the bank, allowing you to make more than 1000% return on your money. This is a no-brainer.

Where else can you get 1000% return on your money, guaranteed, without risk or taxes? All those dentists who have student loans must focus on paying off this debt quickly—especially those who are paying high interest rates. If you paid an additional $3,888 per month, your increased payment would be $6,068 per month, and you would pay the loan off in five years, thus saving $420,835, or about $550,000 before taxes. This is the best deal ever. The reality: If you decided not to pay off the loan in five years, then during those five years, you would pay $130,825 in payments and only $15,054 would go to pay off the original loan amount.

Albert Einstein once said: "Compound interest is the eighth wonder of the world. He who understands it, earns it . . . **he who doesn't, pays it." Understanding this concept is your secret to creating financial freedom quickly.**

Go to Karl's Mortgage calculator to determine what you are truly paying on your loans. https://www.drcalculator.com/mortgage/old/

Below are two Excel charts that show exactly how much interest you are paying over a certain period of years.

30 year - $300,000 loan - Real interest rates before and after taxes (24% federal, 6% state tax)										
	At the 30 year		At the 20 Year		At the 15 year		At the 10 year		At the 5 year	
		Real rate		Real rate		Real rate		Real rate		Real rate
Interest rate	Real rate	before taxes	Real rate	before taxes	Real rate	before taxes	Real rate	before taxes	Real rate	before taxes
3.50%	181%	258%	105%	150%	72%	103%	45%	64%	21%	31%
4%	225%	322%	127%	182%	86%	123%	52%	75%	25%	35%
5%	337%	481%	179%	255%	117%	167%	69%	99%	32%	45%
6%	486%	694%	242%	346%	153%	219%	88%	126%	39%	56%
7%	686%	980%	319%	456%	196%	280%	109%	155%	47%	67%
8%	954%	1363%	414%	592%	245%	350%	132%	188%	56%	79%

	30 years		20 Years		15 years		10 years		5 years	
Interest rate	interest	principal	interest	principal	interest	principal	interest	principal	interest	principal
3.50%	$10,408	$5,757	$ 8,280	$7,885	$ 6,774	$9,391	$ 4,981	$11,184	$2,846	$13,320
4%	$11,904	$5,283	$ 9,619	$7,568	$ 7,947	$9,240	$ 5,904	$11,282	$3,411	$13,776
5%	$14,899	$4,426	$12,391	$6,935	$10,425	$8,900	$ 7,904	$11,422	$4,667	$14,659
6%	$17,900	$3,684	$15,270	$6,313	$13,068	$8,516	$10,097	$11,486	$6,090	$15,494
7%	$20,903	$3,047	$18,239	$5,711	$15,854	$8,097	$12,473	$11,478	$7,679	$16,272
8%	$23,909	$2,506	$21,279	$5,136	$18,763	$7,652	$15,015	$11,401	$9,430	$16,985

DEBT IS THE DEVIL

It's all about net worth. Our net worth is the total of all our assets, including our investments, bank accounts, and real estate, minus our debts. Paying off debt increases your net worth (wealth) and provides an asset that you can use in emergencies as loan collateral. Paying off debt is a conservative investment strategy. So don't be happy about having more tax deductions, especially when you can't write them off, due to the high standard deduction. This is how the government and the banks keep you in debt and in servitude.

Debt keeps you imprisoned and prevents you from living a life of freedom, independence and choice. Being overburdened with financial responsibilities increases your stress, can damage important and satisfying personal relationships, and even lead to divorce, which could cost half of what you own. By changing your spending and saving habits one step at a time, you can regain control of your life. You now know what interest payments really cost you and what to do to change your spending habits.

CREATING A DEBT-FREE OFFICE

Early in my private-practice career, I had a 401(k) plan and even a defined benefit plan. Because the plan was managed by financial advisers and brokers who invested into actively managed funds, the returns were dismal compared to the S&P 500 index fund. Most of my returns went to pay fees to my adviser and the mutual-fund company. I also noticed that, when people left my practice, they would immediately cash in their retirement plan and spend it on something stupid.

Because the returns were so poor with my old plans, I decided to eliminate the retirement plans completely, and give each team member a $250 per month debt-reduction bonus. Each year around Christmas, I give a bonus and have a dinner meeting with my entire team and their spouses; I show them how quickly they can be debt-free using the snowball approach as described in Doctorace.com. I also give each of them my newest book, entitled *The Big Little Book on Creating Personal and Financial Freedom*, published in June 2024.

I encourage my team members to go to **Dave Ramsey's financial peace university**, at https://www.ramseysolutions.com/ramseyplus/financial-peace. Once they complete the program, I would pay for the tuition. Ramsey has also created a great program for your team—called "Smart Dollar"—that is sponsored by you and allows them to have a step-by-step approach to paying off debts. This is one of the best things you can do for your team. It also helps with team retention. https://www.ramseysolutions.com/corporate-wellness/smartdollar

I have created an entire free video program on my website, DoctorAce.com, for doctors and their team to get out of debt.

This debt-reduction approach in my office has been in effect for more than 10 years; I have 6 team members now completely debt-free, including paying off their homes. I have faith that the rest of my team will be completely debt-free within 6 to 10 years. But my greatest gift to them is not being out of debt; my greatest gift is that I changed them from spenders into savers. This has done much to eliminate the money issues that many families argue about. I have recently instituted a low-fee, self-directed, 401(k) plan through Charles Schwab. Here is an example of one of my past team members.

LISA'S STORY

Lisa was my chief clinical assistant and had a small business on eBay. Her husband was making about $20 an hour on his physically demanding construction job. They decided to live on his income and focus everything she earned from my dental office and their eBay business toward debt reduction and paying off their house. Within 4 years, they had paid off their mortgage and were completely debt-free. Their intent is to maximized their solo Roth IRA from her eBay business. For 2024, they have the ability to contribute a combined total of $69,000. By age 65, they could have more than $8,000,000 in their 401(k) Roth, receiving a tax-free passive income of $300,000 per year from dividends.

Once Lisa was debt-free, she left my dental practice. She and her husband work about 15 to 20 hours a week on their eBay business and have plenty of time for travel and enjoying the adventures of life. They had their first child in November. It is surprising how, with strong intent, becoming debt-free happens very quickly.

ELIMINATE ALL DEBT IN THREE TO SIX YEARS

The average American dentist takes home around $200,000 a year after taxes. Most doctors could easily live on $150,000, which gives them $50,000 per year to pay off debt. But with simple modification of some of the practice systems, they could increase their income by an additional $220,000 a year just doing one additional large procedure per day, such as a crown.

If your crown fee is $1,500 and you work 200 days a year, doing an additional crown every day would bring in $300,000 each year. After paying lab fees and materials on the $300,000, you will have made an extra $220,000 from the crowns.

After paying taxes on the $220,000, you will still have an extra $200,000 each year to pay toward reducing debt. Add that to the $50,000 of your original disposable income, and you will have $250,000 to pay off debt. One more crown a day will give you an extra $16,666 each month to pay off debt. Once you are debt-free, you have that additional $20,833 plus your monthly payments of $10,127, equaling $30,960 per month ($371,924 per year) available for investing and your lifestyle. If you invested this $372,000 in dividend-growth stocks every year, you could have $20,000,000 in 20 years and be receiving $600,000 per year in passive income. This is called freedom.

Chapter 4

Achieving Financial Freedom

"THE PROBLEM IN AMERICA isn't so much what people don't know; the problem is what people think they know that just isn't so."—Will Rogers

Everything you have been taught about money makes other people wealthy and keeps you poor. Creating wealth is not complicated! The secret to becoming financially free is to make more money in your practice, quickly pay off debt, receiving a guaranteed 100% tax-free return, and then learn how to maximize your personal investments in a tax-free environment.

These options are never offered to you by your financial advisers because no one makes money from them. What you are offered are risky stocks and mutual funds with high commissions and adviser fees, along with the high anxiety associated with these products. The other supposedly safe type of investment are low-return bonds or treasuries that will never provide adequate passive income for your life.

Most of your advisers will not appreciate this paradigm shift because each of them looks through a different lens, based on their experience, training and what they will make from you.

Each has a different agenda for you and your money. You need to create your own agenda—one that works best for you.

Over the past 50 years, Americans have been taught by banks, the government, financial advisers, and financial institutions to stay in debt while telling them that the only way to become wealthy and retire comfortably is to accept risk, volatility and unpredictability in the stock-market casino through 401(k) plans and other financial vehicles that they control.

These investment models will take away two-thirds of your disposable income and freedom, while keeping you broke, unable to retire, and in debt for the rest of your life. You become their cash cow until you die. This book will help you learn a simple, safe and predictable system to create wealth, obtain your personal and financial freedom, and leave a legacy for your family.

Warren Buffett has said that the late Jack Bogle has probably done more for the American investor than any other person in the country. He is the father of the indexed mutual fund, and he said in *MarketWatch*, "If you pay a hefty fee to an active manager, what happens to your potential return? Answer: Nothing good. A 2.5% fee over a typical investor's lifetime results in an astounding 75% of compounding returns ending up in the hands of the manager, not the investor." Bogle believes that actively managed funds are a big scam.

When you invest in loaded, actively managed mutual funds, you put up 100% of the capital and take 100% of the risk. If you make money, your fund manager takes up to 70% or more of the upside in fees. If you lose money, they still get paid. They are charging you 10 to 30 times what it would cost for you to buy a low-cost index fund that would match the market and beat 90% of the actively managed mutual funds.

Fees of only 1% per year can slash the value of your savings by 28% over the next 35 years, according to the Department of

Labor. These are in addition to other fees in actively managed funds, such as trading costs, taxes, and hidden fees.

Most individual investors put their money in mutual funds and rely upon money managers, financial advisers and brokers who engage in hyperactive trading to try to beat the market by picking winners and timing. This is a losing strategy. More than 96% of investors would be better off consistently investing on their own in an S&P 500 index fund (SWPPX).

Expenses and fees are the enemy of the individual investor. You must understand that advisers, brokers and mutual-fund managers are well-meaning salespeople. If you invest $4,000 per month on your own in an index S&P 500 fund for 30 years at 7% return, you will have earned $3,781,475. With a 1% fee, your financial adviser will take 25% of your earnings over time. With a 2% fee, they will take 46% of your earnings; with a 3% fee, they will take 62% of your earnings; with a 4% fee, they will take 75% of your earnings. Your advisers will always get paid, even when you lose money in market downturns. See the chart below.

Advisory/Fund % fee	The money Advisory/ Fund will take from you	% Return of your earnings
1%	$962,322	25%
2%	$1,725,989	46%
3%	$2,332,220	62%
4%	$2,820,600	75%

"Unfortunately, the vast majority of those who call themselves financial advisers neither charge a fair price nor give good advice. More than any other market I know, the market for financial advice is 'Let the buyer beware.'"

—Jim Dahle, M.D.

THE COST OF ADVISERS

Below is a real example of an actively managed mutual-fund simple IRA compared to the results of the S&P 500 fund over 14 years. In this true example, the individual would have had $706,000 rather than $342,000 (more than twice as much) if they would have just put their investments in the S&P 500 ETF (exchange traded fund).

	BROKERAGE ACCOUNT			RETURNS		S&P 500 ACCOUNT			RETURNS	
YEAR	$ OPEN BAL	$ DEPOSITS	$ PRINCIPAL	%	$	$ OPEN BAL	$ DEPOSITS	$ PRINCIPAL	% PRETAX	$ TREATED
2009	0	7,800	7,800	-0.81%	-63	0	7,800	7,800	26.46%	2,064
2010	7,737	14,950	22,687	5.98%	1,357	9,864	14,950	24,814	15.06%	3,737
2011	24,044	15,400	39,444	-2.44%	-963	28,551	15,400	43,951	2.11%	927
2012	38,481	14,950	53,431	9.99%	5,339	44,878	14,950	59,828	16.00%	9,573
2013	58,770	15,600	74,370	8.56%	6,368	69,401	15,600	85,001	32.39%	27,532
2014	80,738	15,750	96,488	2.86%	2,761	112,532	15,750	128,282	13.69%	17,562
2015	99,249	15,600	114,849	-4.34%	-4,984	145,844	15,600	161,444	1.38%	2,228
2016	109,865	16,900	126,765	6.95%	8,807	163,672	16,900	180,572	11.96%	21,596
2017	135,572	18,650	154,222	12.64%	19,499	202,169	18,650	220,819	21.83%	48,205
2018	173,721	15,654	189,375	-7.26%	-13,751	269,023	15,654	284,677	-4.38%	-12,469
2019	175,624	17,046	192,670	16.67%	32,112	272,209	17,046	289,255	31.49%	91,086
2020	224,782	19,520	244,302	11.24%	27,449	380,341	19,520	399,861	18.40%	73,574
2021	271,751	20,822	292,573	9.37%	27,427	473,435	20,822	494,257	28.71%	141,901
2022	320,000	21,076	341,076	-16.62%	-56,676	636,158	21,076	657,234	-18.11%	-119,025
2023	284,400	21,542	305,942	11.93%	36,503	538,209	21,542	559,751	26.26%	146,991
2024	342,445		342,445			706,742		706,742		

The next real-life example is of a much-larger office that maximized all tax-deductible strategies, including a safe harbor 401(k) with profit sharing. On the left is the true account invested by their financial adviser in mutual funds. On the right is the result if they had invested on their own in the S&P 500 index fund, with an expense ratio of 0.03%. If they just had invested on their own in the S&P 500, they would have had an annual 14.8% return from 2009 to 2025, with an ending balance of more than $5.96 million in their 401(k) account. Compare this to their financial adviser's management of their portfolio, resulting in a final balance of $2.25 million. Over the past 15 years, the plan lost more than $3.7 million (62.2%) by allowing their financial advisers to manage their investments. The doctor just retired at age 65 and wishes he could go back 15 years and take control of his money back then. Each doctor who has a 401(k) needs to do the comparison, and if the results are not as good as the S&P 500, they must learn how to invest safely on their own.

	BROKERAGE ACCOUNT			RETURNS		S&P 500 ACCOUNT			RETURNS	
YEAR	$ OPEN BAL	$ DEPOSITS	$ PRINCIPAL	%	$ GROWTH	$ OPEN BAL	$ DEPOSITS	$ PRINCIPAL	% PRETAX	$ GROWTH
2009	390,507	68,513	459,020	16.64%	76,371	390,507	68,513	459,020	26.46%	121,457
2010	535,391	58,134	593,525	-1.32%	-7,836	580,477	58,134	638,611	15.06%	96,175
2011	585,689	52,811	638,500	-1.60%	-10,197	734,785	52,811	787,596	2.11%	16,618
2012	628,303	66,783	695,086	11.86%	82,423	804,215	66,783	870,998	16.00%	139,360
2013	777,509	83,382	860,891	15.38%	132,374	1,010,357	83,382	1,093,739	32.39%	354,262
2014	993,265	67,551	1,060,816	2.86%	30,377	1,448,002	67,551	1,515,553	13.69%	207,479
2015	1,091,193	73,964	1,165,157	0.89%	10,380	1,723,032	73,964	1,796,996	1.38%	24,799
2016	1,175,537	68,706	1,244,243	5.87%	73,020	1,821,794	68,706	1,890,500	11.96%	226,104
2017	1,317,263	66,839	1,384,102	17.37%	240,416	2,116,604	66,839	2,183,443	21.83%	476,646
2018	1,624,518	72,383	1,696,901	-9.97%	-169,220	2,660,089	72,383	2,732,472	-4.38%	-119,682
2019	1,527,681	74,755	1,602,436	19.13%	306,595	2,612,789	74,755	2,687,544	31.49%	846,308
2020	1,909,031	71,202	1,980,233	9.85%	195,018	3,533,852	71,202	3,605,054	18.40%	663,330
2021	2,175,251	74,212	2,249,463	-1.42%	-31,912	4,268,384	74,212	4,342,596	28.71%	1,246,759
2022	2,217,551	76,300	2,293,851	-16.82%	-385,933	5,589,356	76,300	5,665,656	-18.11%	-1,026,050
2023	1,907,918	84,205	1,992,123	13.22%	263,322	4,639,605	84,205	4,723,810	26.29%	1,241,890
2024	2,255,445		2,255,445			5,965,700		5,965,700		

If you have a 401(k) plan, do a comparison on how your 401(k) plan has done, compared to just investing in the S&P 500 index fund on your own. Do this now, and don't wait until you're ready to retire. Go to: https://www.doctorace.com/resources/ and download the free Excel comparison sheet to see how your investments have done against the S&P 500 fund. Use your annual 5500, which is sent to the IRS each year to fill out this Excel sheet.

To obtain the 5500s, go to: https://www.efast.dol.gov/5500search/ and put in your EIN number to get copies of past 5500s. Go to Part III, 7a to find the-beginning-of-the-year balance and, next to that, the-end-of-the-year balance. The ending balance will be the same for the beginning balance of the next year. Then go to part 8a (1,2,3) to put in the total contributions that year. It is that simple. This will help you realize how much you have lost or gained in your retirement account by using the various advisers and mutual funds.

You can also use this Excel sheet to compare how well your financial adviser has done investing your money in your personal account. Compare your personal investment account to the S&P 500. If the results are poor, you need to transfer your portfolio into an account that you have control of and make your own investment decisions. If this is not possible as an employee in your 401(k), then just put in the employer's match and place it into a low-cost index fund. If you are the employer, you may want to set up or switch over to a self-directed 401(k) plan through Charles Schwab.

Their index funds have no adviser fee or fund fee except a very small expense ratio of 0.02%. Their basic fund setup includes the S&P 500 index fund, US mid-cap index fund, small-cap index fund, international index, bond index fund and treasury inflation-protected securities index fund. Over time, the S&P 500 index fund consistently outperforms all the other funds. Charles Schwab will introduce you to their recommended plan administrator. Phone Schwab at 877-456-0777. https://www.youtube.com/watch?v=W70Vm3RJw_0

Once you have learned to increase your profitability in the practice, you can become completely debt-free in 3 to 6 years. Below are some of the best strategies to safely invest on your own and get the best returns without paying the extraordinarily high fees and commissions of financial advisers and brokers. You'll learn how to invest in the stock market while taking minimal risk simply and safely. Remember, the person who cares the most about your money is you. Learn to invest on your own, and stay away from financial advisers and brokers who work on commission.

"You must unlearn what you have learned."

—Yoda

As Yoda taught in *Star Wars*, the first step is letting go of how you have been programmed in the past. Take charge and control of your own money, and stop playing the bankers', advisers' and financial institutions' game. The new model described in this book will eliminate your money stress and bring peace back into your life.

LEARN HOW TO INVEST SAFELY AND SIMPLY ON YOUR OWN

A verse from the Eagles song "Already Gone," says "So often times it happens that we live our lives in chains, and we never even know we have the key." The key to your personal and financial independence is to get out of debt quickly and learn how to invest in the stock market safely on your own. This can be easily done risk-free through paper trading without the help of a financial adviser and their outrageous management fees. Paper trading will be described below. It is like taking a college course in investing. Is your financial freedom worth this amount of time? In this book, you will be taught a specific game plan to help you reach your investment goals and become financially free.

WHY WE INVEST IN THE STOCK MARKET

Over the past 200 years, the stock market has returned more than 1000 times better than any other investment, including real estate, bonds, treasury bills, gold, or the US dollar. This book will show you how to safely maximize your investment in the stock market. https://pages.stern.nyu.edu/~adamodar/New_Home_Page/datafile/histretSP.html

At the beginning of the annual Berkshire Hathaway meeting in 2018, Warren Buffett wanted to share an important lesson with its shareholders. I will summarize what he said: *"Let's look back to 1942, when I bought my first stock and all the things that have happened since that time. We have had fourteen presidents, seven Republicans and seven Democrats. We had world wars,*

9/11, Cuban missile crisis, and all kinds of terrible events that affected the market. But the best single thing you could have done on March 11, 1942, when I bought my first stock was to buy an index fund (Buffett specifically mentioned the S&P 500 index fund) and never, ever look at another headline. Just like you would have bought a farm and let the tenant farmer run it for you and never sell it. If you had put in $10,000 in an index fund at that time and reinvested the dividends, you would have $51 million today in 2018.

"If you took the same $10,000 and bought 300 ounces of gold, you would have only about $400,000 today. Gold does not produce anything, but businesses do. All you needed to do was to believe America would win the war and America would progress as it has ever since 1776. As America moves forward, American business moves forward. You didn't have to worry what stock to buy or what day to get in or out of the market or what the Federal Reserve would say. You just had to know that America works!" https://www.youtube.com/watch?v=10QoUi2PmNs

Warren Buffett recommends, for those amateur investors who do not want to spend the necessary time researching companies, to just buy a very low-cost S&P 500 index fund every year through thick and thin. Do not try to time the market, but invest a specific amount routinely each month—and never look back. A good example of this is the Charles Schwab S&P 500 Index Fund (SWPPX), which has a very low total expense ratio and no minimum initial investment. One advantage of the S&P 500 is that each year, they get rid of the bad companies and add newer companies that perform well.

Some investors want to equally distribute their cash over the four major indices such as the Dow Jones (DIA), NASDAQ, (QQQ), total stock market index (SWTSX), and S&P 500 (SWPPX). Below is a chart showing their total return over time periods.

Note the low expense ratios especially on the S&P 500 and total stock market index.

Some investors want to equally distribute their cash over the four major indices such as the Dow Jones (DIA), NASDAQ (QQQ), total stock market index (SWTSX), and S&P 500(SWPPX) . Below is a chart showing their total return over time periods. Note the low expense ratios especially on the S&P 500 and total stock market index.

TOTAL RETURNS (JANUARY 2025) (SEEKINGALPHA.COM)

	Expense Ratio	One Year	Three Years	Five Years	Ten Years
NASDAQ (QQQ)	0.20%	26.9%	35.7%	146.5%	**409%**
S&P 500 (SWPPX)	0.02%	27.9%	28.6%	85.2%	**191%**
Dow Jones (DIA)	0.16%	13.7%	21.5%	49.8%	**143%**
Dow Total Stock Market (SWTSX)	0.03%	38.4%	28.1%	81.4%	**174%**

Over the last 100 years, ending in December 2024, the average yearly return of the S&P 500 is 10.54%. This assumes dividends are reinvested. Dividends account for about 40% of the total gain over this period. Adjusted for inflation, the 100-year average stock-market return (including dividends) is 7.4%. For those who start late and have only 15 years before retirement, it's not that easy, through index investing, to reach true financial freedom; they must learn how to invest on their own in individual companies.

The big problem that is overlooked with index investing is stock cycles. There are times when the S&P 500 does not go up at all for many years. These are called "long-term bear markets." The good news is that these bear markets are the best times for value investors to get great buys on wonderful companies through the Rule One investing philosophy, which will be described in Appendix C.

STOCK CYCLES

Alexander's book *Stock Cycles*, published in 2000, reviews the markets over 200 years of American history. During that time, we have had seven long-term bear and seven long-term bull markets. The total average real return in a long-term bull market was 13.2%, while the average return in a long-term bear market was 0.3%.

For example, from 1929 to 1955 (26 years) the annual rate of return on the S&P 500 was only 1.5%. From 1966 to 1982, the total real return was a negative 1.5%. But from 1982 to the year 2000, the average total real return of the market was 18.5%. Alexander then went on to correctly predict that, starting in 2000, there would be a long-term bear market. In March 2013, the price of the S&P 500 was $1527, the same price as it was in March 2000, resulting in a 0.5% annual growth of the S&P 500 index, due to dividends, which is why those 13 years are called "the lost decade."

From January 2010 up until December 2024, the S&P 500 average annual growth was about 13.8%, with reinvestment of dividends. In 2022, the S&P 500 dropped 18.11%, with dividends reinvested. This may have been an indication of the start of a brand-new bear market, but as of today, the market continues to rise.

Recently, there has been a lot of talk about a new recession and the beginning of a new bear market. One indicator of recession has been the recent inversion of the yield curve, when long-term interest rates drop below short-term rates, indicating that investors are moving money away from short-term bonds and into long-term ones. This suggests that the market is becoming more pessimistic about the economic prospects for the near future.

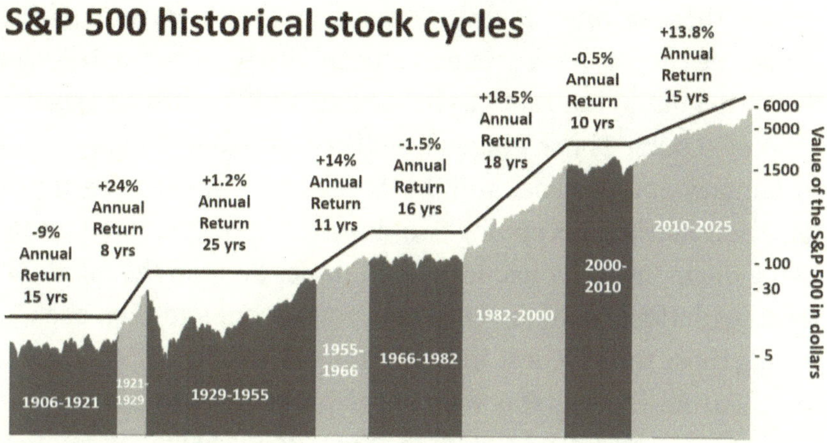

There are three other indicators that show the market is overvalued and that we may be in the beginning of a long, new-term bear market. These are the Buffett Indicator, the Shiller P/E ratio, and the Wilshire GDP. As of **November 2024, the Buffett Indicator value is 208%, approximately (or about 2.0 standard deviation) above the historical trend line**, suggesting that the stock market is strongly overvalued relative to GDP. The Wilshire GDP today is above 195% (extremely overvalued). Dr. Shiller states that, when the P/E ratio of the S&P 500 is low (below 10), the market is undervalued. When the P/E ratio is above 20, the market is overvalued. **In November 2024, the Shiller P/E ratio for the S&P 500 stands at 38.7,** indicating that it would take 38.7 years to get your investment back.

All the above is very interesting, but making investment decisions based on economic predictions is incredibly difficult.

One of the greatest investors of all time, Peter Lynch, said: "It is futile and impossible to try to predict the stock market, interest rates or the economy. If you spend 13 minutes a year on economics, you've wasted 10 minutes." Warren Buffett has also said: "Any firm that hires an economist has one employee too many."

For those of you who do not want to worry about researching companies and getting greater returns, then just buy a low-cost S&P 500 mutual fund such as Schwab (SWPPX), with an expense ratio of 0.02%. The average annual return from January 2010 to January 2025 has been 13.8%. Since 2009, we have been in a long bull market, except for two downturns in 2020 and 2022. Using the monthly indicators of the Charles Schwab *thinkorswim* trading platform could have helped you get out and then back in during those times. These indicators are especially helpful during long bear markets as was seen in the previous example above.

Below is a recent example of the S&P 500 following the monthly arrows of the thinkorswim charts from 2020 to January 2025. Many investors use this chart to determine when the best time is to invest in the S&P 500. They use these 3 up arrows to help them decide when to put more money into the S&P 500. They continue to add to your position as long as the monthly arrows are pointed upwards. When the three monthly arrows Turn downward, they consider moving their money out of the S&P 500 into a money market account until the three monthly arrows reverse upward to move back in. Learn more about thinkorswim trading platform in appendix C.

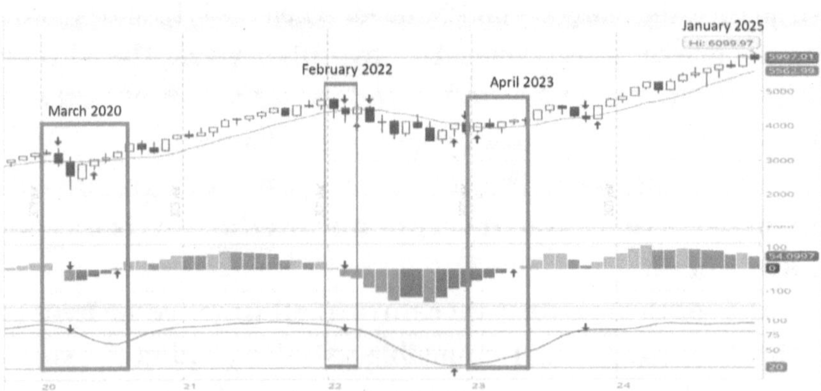

Investing in the stock markets can be the greatest and fastest way to build generational wealth. For those who want to possibly double your returns over that of the S&P 500, you must learn to invest safely on your own without advisors. Do your research on the companies of interest and focus on the underlying fundamentals of the company. Make a watch list, wait, and buy when they go on sale and hold them. Over the long run, the fundamentals are ultimately all that truly matter. Time in the market is more important than timing the market. Many great investors such as Jack Bogle have said, “buy right and hold tight.”

The S&P 500 was at its all-time high in January 2025. During market highs, don’t buy more stocks but build up your cash account and wait for a downturn in the stock market. Today Warren Buffett has almost $325 billion in cash, the highest ever held. Keep the extra cash you add each month to your investment account into a money market account, such as Schwab’s Value Advantage Money Fund—Investor Shares SWVXX paying around 5% today. To help you find the right time to invest, use the three-monthly indicators in the Charles Schwab thinkorswim trading platform.

Bear markets also affect anyone who passively puts their money in the S&P 500 or any mutual fund that matches the market index. Long-term bear markets are the ideal environment for Rule One investors (appendix C). During this time, there are many big ups and downs in the market, when you can buy great companies significantly undervalued. In the last long bear market from 2000 to 2010, the market had two significant drops of 40% and 49% along with increases of 87% and 122%.

S&P 500 return during the lost decade from 2000 to 2013 using thinkorswim 3 arrow indicators

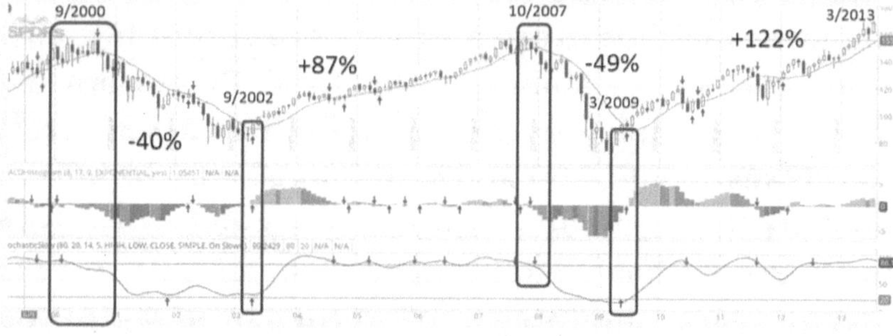

To learn more in-depth knowledge about investing on your own, go to Appendix C.

RETIREMENT ACCOUNTS AND TAXES

To maximize the amount of money you will have, it is very important to place as much as you can in tax-free or deferred tax-free vehicles. Examples of these are: Health Savings Account (HSA), Traditional IRAs, Roth IRAs, SIMPLE IRA Retirement Plans, Safe-Harbor 401(k) Retirement Plan, Safe-Harbor 401(k) Profit-Sharing Retirement Plan, Cash Balance Retirement Plan and Backdoor Roth IRAs. Check out the different tax-deferred and tax-free options: https://www.investopedia.com/. https://www.ruleoneinvesting.com/blog/financial-control/investment-vehicles/. Another site: https://www.irs.gov/retirement-plans/cola-increases-for-dollar-limitations-on-benefits-and-contributions

Since I'm not a tax attorney or CPA, I'm not going to advise you about how to set up these plans. I will tell you I'm not a huge fan of any retirement plan managed by a financial adviser that forces you to invest in mutual funds. The only time a 401(k) is better than an IRA is when the company you work for matches the funds you put in. In that case, take the free money, but put in only the amount they're going to match.

As an employer, you may want to start your own self-directed safe-harbor 401(k) profit-sharing plan through Charles Schwab. This also has a Roth component. The employees will be given a range of different low-cost funds, including a money-market fund. Employers and other senior employees can have the option to self-direct their investments. You and your spouse may be able to put more than $100,000 each year in a Safe-Harbor Roth 401(k) Profit-Sharing Retirement Plan. If funded for the next 20 years, obtaining a 10% return, would give you

$64 million in a tax-free Roth IRA. You could live on that!!! Since March 2009, the average S&P 500 return, with dividends reinvested, has been 15.9%. This rate of return would give you a tax-free portfolio of $144 million after 20 years.

Charles Schwab will introduce you to a plan administrator, who will create the plan design and do the testing of the plan. The cost of setting up the plan and maintaining it ranges between $2000 and $5000 a year, depending on the number of employees. You can call Schwab at 877 456-0777. If you do have a 401(k) plan now, compare how well your advisers have done compared to the S&P 500, as described previously in this book. If you are not happy with your high-fee, wealth-adviser-run plan, you can easily move it to a self-directed plan through Schwab. https://www.youtube.com/watch?v=W70Vm3RJw_0

Solo 401(k): If you are self-employed (one-person outfit, a freelancer, or an independent contractor) and don't employ others, you can have a solo 401(k), also known as an independent 401(k) plan. Couples running businesses together also qualify. You can contribute to your solo 401(k) as both employer and employee. For 2025, you can contribute a combined total of $70,000. If you're 50 or older, you can add another $7,500. In 2025, people ages 60 to 63 get a higher catch-up contribution of $11,250. You can choose between a traditional plan or a Roth plan. I highly recommend that you make it a Solo Roth 401(k). https://www.investopedia.com/ask/answers/100314/do-i-need-employer-set-401(k)-plan.asp

If you have money in a standard tax-deferred 401(k), you can convert all or part of the money into a Roth 401(k). When you do this, you will need to pay the tax on the money transferred at the end of the year, when you receive your 1099. Would you rather pay the tax on $100,000 now or pay 50% tax on it as it grows to $3,000,000 in 20 years or $15,000,000 over the 30 years? This should not be a hard question to answer. Once your standard 401(k) is converted into a Roth 401(k), you will never pay any tax on the gains or withdrawal of the money.

Everyone should have a Roth IRA. If you make too much money for a Roth IRA, then open a standard IRA account, and fund the maximum allowable amount that year. Once funded into the account, you can then transfer that money into a backdoor Roth IRA and pay the taxes.

Roth IRAs are tax-free forever! You put the money in after you pay tax on it, and it grows inside the Roth tax-free, and then, when you retire and take it out, you never have to pay tax on the gains. Teach your children how to invest using Rule One philosophy as you help them open and learn how to invest in their own Roth IRA account. Dave Ramsey tell you why Roth investments are better than traditional. https://www.youtube.com/watch?v=SeRia5tP_Ws

Any online brokerage can help you set up a Roth IRA over the phone. It's easy and takes only a few minutes. This can also show you how to roll over a 401(k) that's no longer being matched by your employer. (Your accountant can help you determine which one is best for you, as well as how much you can allocate to it on an annual basis.)

Simple IRAs are also excellent. You can pack away a huge amount every year tax-free if you qualify. The key thing is to get the money into a tax-deferred or tax-free Roth account. Not all the money we have to invest will be able to be put in a tax-free account. Some of the money you're investing might be in a taxable account.

When you become debt-free and have learned to invest through paper trading, you will create such an abundance, most of which will probably be in a taxable account. I don't mind being in the highest tax bracket because it means I'm making the most money. Nathan Winklepleck, CFA, has a YouTube video that talks about retiring early and paying no taxes. https://www.youtube.com/watch?v=e4ocpTaWNdU

To count on having a comfortable life and a secure future in retirement, you must learn to invest on your own. This will ensure the maximum return on the money you have to invest. Passing on this responsibility to financial advisers to help you invest your savings could result in losing half or more of your retirement income.

TAX STRATEGIES TO HELP YOU REDUCE OR ELIMINATE ALL TAXES ON YOUR INVESTMENTS

Investors must pay taxes on their dividends, but how much they pay depends on their income and whether the dividends are "qualified" or "ordinary." Some realty companies (REITs) that pay dividends are non-qualified, such as Getty Realty (GTY), and you pay your standard tax rate.

Qualified dividends receive more favorable tax treatment but must meet a few criteria. They must be issued by a US corporation that is publicly traded on major exchanges and indices, such as S&P 500, Dow Jones or NASDAQ. Most dividends from US companies are qualified but only if you own the stock for more than 60 days during the 121-day period that begins 60 days before the ex-dividend date.

The ex-dividend date, otherwise called the "ex-date," typically comes one or two business days ahead of the record date. The record date is the day on which the company checks its records to identify shareholders of the company. An investor must be listed on that date to be eligible for a dividend payout that quarter. Therefore, to be eligible for dividends, you must buy or own the stock at least one business day before the ex-dividend date.

The dividend payout date, also known as the "pay date" or the "payable date," is the day on which a declared stock dividend is scheduled to be paid (mailed out) to eligible investors. This date can be up to a month after the ex-dividend date. To find these key dates for your individual companies, go to your Schwab account, and click on the stock symbol. To verify that you received your dividends, go to your Schwab account, and click "history" up on top. This will show you all your account transactions, including dividend payouts.

The tax rates for ordinary (non-qualified) dividends (typically those that are paid out from most common or preferred stocks) are the same rates as you pay on regular income, such as salary or wages. This ranges somewhere between 10% and 37% for the 2025 tax year, depending on your income. Income-tax and capital-gains rates change over time, but in recent years, capital gains rates have been substantially lower.

Currently, the 2025 tax schedule for qualified dividends features only three levels:

Those who earn less than a sum of $48,350 annually or are in the 10% and 12% tax brackets pay no taxes on their dividend income. If your income is below $96,700 for a married couple filing jointly, you will probably not owe any taxes on your dividend income.

Single taxpayers earning more than $48,351 up to $533,400 and married couples filing jointly who earn from $96,701 up to $600,050 are in the 22%, 24%, and 32% tax brackets. They pay their taxes on dividends at only a 15% tax rate.

Individuals earning $533,401 or more and married couples earning more than $600,051 are in the 35% or 37% tax bracket. They will pay only 20% of their annual dividend income in taxes. When the taxes are paid, you will get a step-up basis by Schwab on those stocks where you reinvested your dividends.

There is an additional 3.8% Net Investment Income Tax (NIIT) on investment gains or income. The IRS uses the lowest figure of net investment income or the excess of the modified adjusted gross income (MAGI) that exceeds $200,000 for single filers, $250,000 for married filing jointly, and $125,000 for married filing separately to determine this tax.

This tax is assessed regardless of whether the dividends received are classified as qualified or ordinary. The Net Investment Income Tax is an additional 3.8% tax that applies to dividend income (as well as realized gains) and increases the effective total tax rate on dividends and other investment income.

Learn more about current dividend tax rates: https://www.nerdwallet.com/article/taxes/dividend-tax-rate#Dividend%20tax%20rate%202025

Yet, even with this surcharge, qualified dividends are taxed at significantly better rates versus regular income or short-term capital gains. That doesn't reduce the risk of investing in the stock, but it does offer the prospect of keeping more of your hard-earned gains for yourself.

When you are buying dividend stocks in your tax-deferred account, such as a 401(k) or conventional IRA, you do not pay taxes on your reinvested dividend income that year. Instead, you will pay taxes on your compounded gains once you start to withdraw money in your retirement. The great exception to this is if you are in a Roth IRA. Unlike a 401(k) or IRA, where your cash deposits into the account are made with pre-tax dollars, all your cash deposits into a Roth IRA account are made with after-tax dollars, and so you never pay income tax on withdrawals or gains made in the future.

Every year in February, Charles Schwab will send you a document called a "1099." They will also send a copy to the IRS. This 1099 will tell you how much dividend income you collected in the previous year, so that you can calculate your taxes on it. Again, be sure to consult with a tax professional (which I am not).

THE 5 COMMON MISTAKES YOU NEED TO AVOID WHILE PLANNING FOR RETIREMENT

The **first** mistake is not understanding how much you're going to need to retire. During retirement, you may have fewer expenses in some areas, but other areas, such as healthcare and travel, will increase. Also, inflation will affect the buying power of your nest egg. Check out the investment calculator at: https://www.ruleoneinvesting.com/investment-calculators/

The **second** mistake is relying on fund managers and advisers, who could take up to 70% of your return in fees over time. You have the tools you need to learn to invest on your own on the Internet. The **third** mistake is not taking advantage of your employer 401(k) matching money. Don't invest any more than is matched unless you have the ability to self-direct in investments that you understand. The **fourth** mistake is over-diversifying in many companies through mutual or index funds. Warren Buffett says "Diversification is a protection against ignorance. It makes very little sense for those who know what they're doing." Focus on owning 6 to 15 individual wonderful companies that you understand and like. **But if you are not interested in learning how to invest on your own, then Warren Buffett recommends the S&P 500 index fund, as described above, as probably being your best choice.**

The **fifth** mistake is not researching these companies thoroughly and failing to understand the true intrinsic value so that you can purchase them at Margin of Safety price. In the three-day Rule One Zoom course, they will teach you how to determine true intrinsic value and use the toolbox to find the optimal purchase price.

Investing in great companies is the best hedge against inflation and can be the best and safest place to put your money to beat inflation. Over the past 20 years, the inflation rate has been around 2.8%. In 2022, we had the highest inflation rate in 40 years, spiking to 9%. In September 2024, the inflation rate was 3.3%, with no indication that it would fully subside soon.

If we could just buy and hold, there wouldn't be a tax issue. But sooner or later, we will want to spend the money. The big advantage of using the *thinkorswim* tools and three-arrow indicators is to help us get in and out of the market, with the big guys allowing us to make money while reducing the chance of losing money. The problem is that, when that money is in a taxable account, there can be long-term or short-term capital-gains taxes. If you plan to sell a company, try to hold it for at least a year and a day so that you will have long-term capital gains.

It is still better to make and keep your gains (profits) earned in the market and sell, even if you must pay taxes. The strongest lesson we learn from Rule One investing is that we can keep our excess money working for us through one-week to one-month option trading, but we will have to pay taxes. I would rather make 20 to 25% gains and pay taxes on it, versus making 0% and paying no taxes. Remember, when your cash is in a money-market account, you will still be paying taxes on the interest earned.

SHOULD YOU BUY OR RENT A HOME?

Bottom line: Do not purchase a home until your student loans are all paid off and you have at least a 20% down payment. The average American moves every 7 years. By then, only 12% of the home is paid off with a 30-year mortgage. Then they get a new mortgage, starting all over again at 100%.

With a $280,000 mortgage over those 7 years, they have paid only $34,257 toward their mortgage principal, and lost $90,569 to the bank in interest. They also paid an additional 6% in sales commission ($16,800), $10,000 in home improvements, plus $4,000 in closing costs. **The bottom line: there was no increase in their net worth, and they will never get out of debt.**

If they stay in the home and choose to pay back the original $280,000 loan at 4.9 % over the next 30 years, they will pay the $280,000 home price plus the $254,972 in interest, which equals $534,972 in after-tax money. I recommend that you never carry a mortgage larger than twice your gross income, and you should not spend more than 16% to 20% of your gross income on housing, including your mortgage payment, utilities, property tax, insurance and maintenance.

Buy a home that is just large enough for your family and that you can afford to pay off in seven to ten years. Make sure that you get a mortgage that has no penalty or fee for paying it off early. If you pay off the $280,000 home in seven years, you would need to pay only $51,225 in interest and would save an additional $203,647 that would've gone to interest. Now you can use this money to invest in your retirement plan. Check out: https://www.drcalculator.com/mortgage/old/

Remember: when buying a home over thirty years, most of the mortgage payments initially go to interest, and very little goes to the principal (ownership) to pay off the home. For the first fifteen years, it is just like renting, except you have all the additional property taxes, maintenance and homeowner's insurance. Beyond that, in most cases you can't even write off the interest on your taxes because they are less than the standard deduction. You are much better off renting until you have a 20% down payment (to eliminate the need for private mortgage insurance) and can plan to pay off the house in seven to ten years.

Focus all excess money on those payments, and don't dilute your extra money by paying into children's college fund or into your retirement unless it's matched by your employer. Once you are debt-free and have maximized your retirement funding, then you can invest in your children's college funding.

When you buy a home, you now have real estate in your portfolio, and it becomes a form of forced savings, just like a long-term inflation-adjusted bond. And once it has been paid off, the money that went to your mortgage payment now can be used to invest in wonderful companies. Your paid-off home also becomes a safety net, from which equity can be used in emergencies through home-equity loans.

The choice between buying a home and renting one is among the biggest financial decisions that many adults make. I would recommend renting if you do not plan to live in the house for longer than seven years. Go to: https://www.whitecoatinvestor.com, and type in "Should I buy or rent?"

Get rid of private mortgage insurance (PMI). If you did not have a 20% down payment when you purchased your house, you had to buy PMI, or private mortgage insurance. This is very expensive and a waste of money. It can cost you up to 1% of the loan amount annually. A $400,000 house will require $4,000 a year in insurance payments, or $333 in monthly payments. In accordance with the Homeowners Protection Act of 1998, your lender must terminate PMI on the date your loan balance is scheduled to reach 78% of the original value of your home (in other words, when your equity reaches 22%, provided you are current on your mortgage payments).

Call your lender and ask them to cancel your PMI when you have paid down the mortgage balance to 80% of the home's original appraised value. You might have to write your lender a cancellation letter for the PMI. Accelerate your payments as fast as you can to eliminate the PMI, and, once you've done this, you'll have an additional $333 a month to pay off your home early. https:/ www.investopedia.com/mortgage/insurance/how-get-rid-pmi

ESTATE-PLANNING AND ASSET-PROTECTION CHECKLIST

Statistics show that, in 2023, about 25% of 18- to 54-year-olds have a will. 45% of people over the age of 55 have a will. 81% of people over the age of 72 have a will, and only 18% were living trusts. James, my dental assistant of 19 years, died suddenly from a heart attack while golfing at age 37, without a will and with extensive assets. His estate will need to go through probate and all the time, attorney fees and other expenses associated with that process.

We just do not know when things will happen. It is also very important to have power of attorney for finance and healthcare directives. When you are debt-free and have investments, you need to protect them and ensure they are passed down to your family with very little tax and no probate or attorney fees.

Without these items, there is a great possibility that, if something happens to you and your spouse, your drunken brother will take over all the money, spend it, and throw your kids out onto the street. Think about it. Without a revocable living trust, your estate will go into probate, which makes all your assets public and is very expensive and emotionally draining to your heirs. It could take years before your estate is settled, thus depleting much of your estate's assets because they are going to attorney fees.

I was working with a thirty-four-year-old dentist who was married and had a little girl and another child on the way. I told him to go to his local attorney and get these estate-planning documents drawn up. He said he would. Six months later, he was coming with his wife and team to one of my seminars in Seattle. During the flight, the plane had a landing-gear issue, and they thought they would have to make a crash landing in Seattle. Fortunately, they got the gear down and landed safely. At the meeting, I asked him, "Don't you feel better now that you have your asset-protection plan in place?" He sheepishly said, "I will get those things done as soon as I get back."

Find a local attorney, and get these things done now:

- Durable power of attorney for healthcare
- Durable power of attorney for finances
- Living will
- Standard will
- Revocable living trust

For a less-expensive approach, you can also go to LegalZoom.com and set up a will and power of attorneys for as little as $200 with the help of their attorneys. https://www.legalZoom.com/personal/estate-planning/estate-planning-bundle.

Make sure to update beneficiaries on all your banking and investment accounts. The beneficiaries get first claim, and those listed in the will are secondary. Create a trust, and put all your taxable personal-investment accounts and home in the name of the trust. Do not put your automobiles in the trust due to possible legal actions during a suit. Also do not put your 401(k), IRAs, Annuities or life insurance in your trust because they already have designated beneficiaries. The trust itself could be one of the beneficiaries in your 401(k), IRAs, Annuities and life insurances. Fill out a document locator that shows all of your assets and the location of all important documents, such as your wills, trusts, brokerage account and passwords. List the names, phone numbers and emails of all important people, such as your accountant, attorney, banker and friends. All this and other important information should be given to someone you trust, such as your spouse, parents or sibling, in case something happens to you and/or your spouse. This will be an important document for your family. You can download a free document locator at: https://doctorace.com/resources/

Just buy cheap term life insurance that will cover you until you are debt-free and have created a portfolio of investments that can give you and your family passive income for life.

Health insurance is very important for financial security. An illness/sickness can destroy you and your financial well-being for a decade or more. Try to be under your parents' health insurance until you are at least 26 years old. Find a job that provides health insurance.

FINANCIAL MYTHS

Over the years, we have been imprinted with financial myths. Once we look closely at them, we realize how they are wrong and keep us from reaching our financial goals. Below, I will address a few of these beliefs and recommend you see them for what they are: myths.

Myth 1: Good debt versus bad debt. Some people say that your house or your business are good debt. But all debt is bad and sucks the life out of your financial world. We must remember that debt is the devil! Get rid of it as soon as possible. Becoming debt-free uncomplicates your life.

Myth 2: Pay yourself first, and start saving for your retirement. The problem with doing this is that you're only getting less than 1% return in your savings account, when, instead, you could use that money and get more than a 100% return right now by paying off debt, which is the fastest way to become wealthy.

Myth 3: Why pay off a 3% interest rate home loan when I can make 7% investing? We must remember it's not a 3% interest rate for the first year of a 30-year mortgage but a

200% interest rate. Paying off the principal payment of your debt can give you more than a 100% return, guaranteed, without risk. And again, who says we are going to get 7% in the market? In some years, the market has dropped by 35%.

Myth 4: Buy the most expensive house you can afford. This just keeps you in debt longer and adds many more expenses to your life. The more expensive the house, the more you will pay in property taxes, home maintenance, home upgrades, yard maintenance and (if you live in such a neighborhood) community dues. You now must upgrade your lifestyle to keep up with the neighbors. Instead, buy someone else's dream house that fits your needs. You will save 20% versus building your own house and sidestep the headaches of construction.

Dr. Doug Carlson says that home maintenance, property taxes and upgrades average 2% of your home's value per year for a modest home. Thus, a $500K home will need $10,000 per year. Unfortunately, that peripheral cost of 2% will increase with a more-expensive home. Often, you'll pay 3% for a $1.5M home and more than 4% for a $2M+ home. Yes, doctors can pay $80K or more each year for their "trophy" home.

Dr. James M. Dahle, the author of *The White Coat Investor*, gives some good reasons why renting a home has its advantages during certain times in your career. Go to: https://www.white-coatinvestor.com and type in "Should I buy or rent?"

Myth 5: Emergency-fund myth. Some financial advisers recommend saving three to six months of living expenses in an emergency fund before you start paying off debt. The problem with this approach is that you never get around to paying off the debt, because it takes about two years to save up that amount, and, meanwhile, many people take out the money for non-emergency items. You must begin to see debt as a tax and automatically pay 10% to 20% of your monthly income toward your debt. Once your credit cards are paid off, if you do have an emergency fund, you can get a line of credit or a home-equity loan—or you can just stop paying those accelerated payments for one or two months.

Myth 6: The budgeting myth. Again, many good financial advisers recommend you observe where you're spending your money and then budget so much each month, which allows you to set aside money to pay off debts. The problem is that this gives you a false sense of security, and there is usually nothing left at the end of the month. The secret of debt elimination is to automatically take 10% to 20% out of your bank account each month to pay off debt as if it were a tax. I can guarantee you that, if you take 10% to 20% out each month and pay it toward debt, you will be broke at the end of the month just like you are now, except that you will be well on your way to becoming debt-free.

Myth 7: College-funding myth. Many people recommend that you start funding your child's education early, so that you have enough when they're ready for school. They might recommend 529 plans that are run by different states, which have high-load, actively managed funds. The returns are dismal. You also have less control over the money. It is better to focus on debt reduction and, when debt-free, you can easily fund your children's college education with cash. When you are debt-free and you want to start a 529 plan, check out savingforcollege.com for the best plans in all states.

Myth 8: The "more money" myth. I've heard so many doctors say, "If I just had more money. . . ." When I first began my coaching program, I showed dentists how to make more money, but I forgot to teach them about getting out of debt. They just got into larger amounts of debt and are now trapped in their large homes and large, high-stress lives. More money will not make you happy, but if you are focused on eliminating your debt, your life will become much more stress-free.

Myth 9: Life insurance as an investment. One of the worst investments that you can make in terms of the amount of return you get is from a whole-life insurance policy. Dave Ramsey calls whole-life insurance the "payday loan of the middle class." But if you are a spender and are unable to pay off debt or save anywhere else, it might be right for you. Insurance is there only to protect your family when you do not have enough assets. Additional reading: H. Andrew Tobias' book *The Only Investment Guide You Ever Need* helps you determine how much life insurance you really need.

Myth 10: Monthly payments are normal. Our culture has taught us that we always need to be in debt. This makes a lot of money for many people in the banking and investment industries. So, stop paying them 100% interest.

Myth 11: Avoid-paying-taxes myth. Dentists lose money by trying different schemes to prevent paying taxes. You should want to pay more taxes than any other dentist, because it indicates you are making more money than any other dentist. Rely on your CPA. A good CPA will keep you honest and make sure you don't give more to the government than you need to.

Myth 12: Financial-adviser myth. There is an old saying, "A broker will invest your money until you are broke." In the past, it was much more complicated to invest in the markets, because people had to go to different brokerage houses and work through brokers. With the internet, it is easy to create an account online and find low-load index funds that will beat 96% of all the financial advisers because of the minimal 1% to 3% to manage your investments. Remember, a 1% advisory fee could cost you $1.5 million over twenty years if you had a $1.2 million 401(k) and you contributed $72,000 per year with an 8% return. For non-retirement money, use the free Schwab advisers, and contribute each month into the S&P 500 index fund.

Myth 13: Myth of bi-weekly mortgage payments. It is true that paying your mortgage twice a month will cause a 30-year mortgage to be paid off in about twenty-two years and save 25% of the interest. This strategy creates a false sense of security and keeps you from quickly getting totally out of debt, including paying off the home, in five to seven years and saving 80% of the interest.

Myth 14: Don't pay off your house early because you can write off the interest rate on your taxes. One of the biggest misconceptions that banks and accountants perpetuate is that you should not pay off your house early because you can write off the interest on your taxes. If we look at this closely, in 2024 an average American couple who pays $10,000 a year in interest has the choice of taking the standard deduction of $29,200 or to itemize their return and take the $10,000 tax write-off. When they itemize, they are unable to take the standard deduction of $29,200 and have an overall loss of $14,000. The standard deduction in 2024 filing separately—$14,600. Married Filing Jointly or Qualifying Surviving Spouse—$29,200. Head of Household—$21,900.

AVOIDING FINANCIAL MISTAKES

Warren Buffett said, "The first rule of investment is, don't lose money. The second rule of investment is, never forget rule number one." The most important way to keep your wealth is to never make a big financial mistake. Big financial mistakes usually occur because of greed and ego. I have known numerous dentists who have lost their entire portfolio in a get-rich-quick scheme. Such schemes range from real-estate deals to limited partnerships; they can take the form of just about anything else that sounds too good to be true.

Remember, there is no free lunch. When you have a systematic guide to get out of debt, increase your practice profitability, and conservatively invest in the US market, then you will become economically free in a fairly short time. Why take a risk on anything else? If you just stick with the boring Dr. Ace's Financial Freedom philosophy of investing, you'll never put your retirement money at risk. **Here are some other financial mistakes that you should avoid.**

Not stopping to find out what makes you happy. The things that really make me happy are very simple and cost almost nothing. If I had known this earlier at the deepest level, I would not have needed to drive myself so hard to be successful. This is why the process of writing a new story is so important. Write down what you want your average day to look like. What are the things that make you happy? (Don't include shopping!) What are the happiest times you've enjoyed in your life?

When you know who you are, it is easy to save money. Usually, the simplest and least-expensive things make you happy. Try to spend the least amount of money trying to figure out what makes you happy. Rent your way through the discovery process (for example, rent that lovely condo in the mountains rather than buy it). Most people live a life of high debt and stress because they spend money, hoping it will make them happy. I guarantee that more money or things will not give you peace or happiness.

Allowing our ego to ruin our lives by creating an unconscious compulsion to enhance one's identity through association with and purchase of expensive items, e.g., jewelry, exotic cars and luxury homes. Yet rarely do these purchases satisfy the ego desires that make it feel different and special.

Lending money to friends and family. If you lend money to friends or family, please realize there is a good possibility you will never be repaid. Often this has a negative impact on the relationship. If lending the money is meaningful to you, then consider simply giving it as a gift. Never cosign a loan; in most cases, you will end up paying the loan. A cosigner is a fool with a pen.

Falling for get-rich-quick schemes and scams. Never get involved in any investment that you don't completely understand.

With this guide, you do not have to take risks. You already have it made. When you are asked to invest in something new, just tell them that you invest only in no-load S&P 500 or the US stock market, but thanks anyway. Check out: https://www.whitecoat-investor.com/12-rules-to-help-you-avoid-getting-scammed/

Listening to investment financial advisers who say they can beat the market. Only a fool would say they can beat the market, so just stick with no-load index funds that you have researched and can buy yourself.

Getting into a limited partnership. You lose control as a limited partner and are the last to be paid. Stay away from any investment or thing that you do not understand thoroughly or do not have personal control of decisions over. I knew one doctor that lost his entire retirement savings of $300,000 in a limited partnership that it took him 20 years to accumulate.

Living in a high-cost, high-congestion and high-tax area. If you to work and live in a large city like San Francisco or New York City, where homes can be two to three times more expensive, you will find that traffic is terrible and that there are high state and city taxes that can delay your becoming debt-free and financially free. Think about moving to a tax-free state such as Texas, Florida, Wyoming, Washington, Alaska, New Hampshire, South Dakota, Tennessee or Nevada. Live in a smaller, safer, less-expensive and less-hectic community. You will be able to buy a nicer and bigger home that you can pay off in five to seven years.

Buying too big a house. Consider what you really need. Buying a bigger house than you need wastes money monthly. The cost of your home should not exceed two times your gross salary.

Buying a vacation home or large boat that you rarely use. If this adds meaning to your life and you use it often, like more than sixty days a year, then it is worth the investment. That is, until it no longer adds meaning to your life—and at that time, you can sell it. It is not a bad idea for some properties like vacation homes or boats to be shared with other owners to dilute the expenses.

Buying timeshares. Never buy them. You have a greater selection and a much-lower price if you go to vacation rental by owner (VRBO.com).

Buying annuities. Never buy them.

Starting another business before you start making your own practice successful. A well-run dental practice can be one of the most successful businesses on this planet. Maintain your focus, and start having fun again in your practice.

Marry the wrong person. Stay away from spenders. Find someone who is conservative in their spending habits and has financial goals similar to yours. Marry the right person the first time.

Not getting a prenuptial agreement if you have assets. Get your spouse (male or female) to sign on the dotted line before you say, "I do."

Having too many "successful" marriages. Before divorcing, try to reinvent your relationship, and work through a counselor to see if you can make the relationship work. If there is no possibility of working it out, then you both deserve your freedom. There's often a lot of anger and trying to "get even" in the divorce process. I recommend that you offer your spouse a generous settlement and treat them with kindness and respect.

Always try to maintain strong relationships with your children; never put down your partner. If your spouse wants more and does not accept your generous offer, then tell your attorney that his or her job is simply to get you in front of the judge and no longer communicate with your spouse's attorney. This will save both of you a lot of money in attorney fees. Judges are normally fair in their settlements. If you continue to marry the same type of person (alcoholic, codependent, crazy), then this is the time for some personal growth and counseling. One group I work with who are exceptionally good in helping individuals to identify, address and let go of these issues is Legacy Life Consulting. Contact them at: https://www.legacylifeconsulting.com/ David Stamation (208) 946-3894.

Be sure to check out: https://www.whitecoatinvestor.com/stupid-doctor-tricks-biggest-financial-mistakes/

FINAL THOUGHTS ON INVESTING

Learning to invest on your own and creating wealth is not complicated! First learn how to make more money in your work and quickly pay off debt. During this time, learn how to invest using paper money as described in Rule One investing. Also fund your Roth IRA each year. You may have to use the backdoor Roth technique to do so. To help you through this process, check out my June 2024 book entitled: *The Big Little Book on Creating Personal and Financial Freedom.*

Evaluate how you and your adviser's investments have done compared to the S&P 500 over time. Go to: https://www.doctorace.com/resources/ and download the free Excel comparison sheet to see how your investments have done against the S&P 500 fund. If you have not done as well as the S&P 500, then you must learn to invest correctly on your own following the Rule One investing strategy. Open a brokerage account through Charles Schwab, and download the *thinkorswim* trading platform to learn how to paper trade.

Read the books by Phil Town, and go to his website ruleoneinvesting.com to learn how to find wonderful companies. I highly recommend that you take their $97.00 three-day Zoom investment course.

Create a watch list of wonderful companies by using the stock scanner on the Rule One toolbox. These are the businesses you want to own and that you will buy if the price is right. Your watch list can contain more than 20 stocks. Eventually, you will own the best 6 to 15 companies from your initial watch list.

When evaluating companies for your watch list, look for three things. The first and maybe the most important is return on invested capital (ROIC). This is the earnings of the capital divided by all capital in the company. We would like to see it 20% or higher. The next is evaluating the company's debt. Ideally, we would like a company that has no debt or less than one year of debt. The last thing we look at is cash flow. This is determined by looking at the income statement. Free cash flow is determined by subtracting the operating cash flow from that of the capital expenditures. We want free cash flow of at least 10% or higher.

Sit back and relax. Only buy companies on sale. You wait for an event either in the economy, industry or with the company itself. You need to be patient. You make money when you wait. Always buy a stock at a big margin of safety. Buying low and selling when they're very high can make you wealthy.

Most of our investment time is just doing nothing and waiting for the right event. You need to look at your portfolio only once a month, when you have added money into your account, to put in the 5% money-market account, or to buy more stocks. Other than that, **you should not** be even thinking about your portfolio or what the market is doing. Warren Buffett once said, "Lethargy bordering on sloth remains the cornerstone of our investment style."

Whatever you decide to do, the most important thing is to just get started. You don't have to wait for a big downturn in the market. The sooner you start investing in dividend stocks or a 5% money-market fund, the sooner you will start building wealth and creating passive income. Time is the greatest advantage that you can have in the stock market. If you combine compounding with time, you have the perfect recipe for building generational wealth.

Chapter 5

Enjoy Life, Liberty and the Pursuit of Happiness

Enjoying Good Health

ABOUT SIX YEARS AGO, I noticed that my computer IT guy had lost a considerable amount of weight. He was six foot two, and when I first met him, he weighed around 300 pounds. Within six months, he had dropped 100 pounds and now looked great. I was amazed because I disliked exercise and had always had trouble losing weight, so I asked him what his secret was.

He told me that weight loss was pretty much 90% diet and 10% exercise. He said he changed his eating habits and moved to a high-fat, low-carbohydrate, ketogenic method of eating. He recommended a site called Dietdoctor.com, which was founded in 2011 and has more than 80,000 members worldwide, making it the largest low-carb site in the world. It is filled with many articles, experts, videos and low-carb recipes.

At that time, I was five foot six and weighed about 210 pounds, with a beautiful potbelly. Within three months of taking his advice, I lost more than 45 pounds and have maintained my weight at 165 pounds for the past eight years. I walk a couple of miles once a week and do some weightlifting three times a week to keep my muscle tone. I take multivitamins, vitamin D, magnesium, and fish oil. I can now sleep eight hours a night, and I feel better than I have for years.

Another great website to help transform your health is http://drhyman.com/. Dr. Mark Hyman is an American physician and a *New York Times* bestselling author. He is the founder and medical director of the Ultra Wellness Center and director of the Cleveland Clinical Center for Functional Medicine.

CREATING GREAT RELATIONSHIPS

Warren Buffett gives the following advice: *"Be around people that you admire and enjoy. They usually have an upbeat attitude about life, they're humorous, have integrity and are generous people who think about what they can do for you. These qualities that you admire are not innate at birth, and you can acquire them. Then there are those negative qualities that turn you off in people who always need to be right and that you don't enjoy being with.*

You can choose what person you want to be, so why not choose the person you admire? Take your five best friends, mentors, or your heroes, and write down the qualities that you like about them. Incorporate these qualities into your life and eliminate the qualities of the people that turn you off. It's that simple. It is important to work with people in your life, and you will get the best out of people if they like you. You need to develop these habits now. Incorporate the great qualities now and eliminate the bad qualities, and you will have an incredible life. Choose your heroes very carefully because they will define you. You are one of your children's favorite heroes."

Buffett also said that the secret to long-lasting relationships is low expectations. A friend told me that relationships improve immensely when you give up the need to be right. Re-evaluate your community by listing the top 5 people you spend time with, and ask, *Do those relationships add to my future self?*

Picking the right partner can be one of the most important financial decisions you'll ever make. Having too many successful marriages (divorces) can destroy your finances. Too many times, we get out of relationships for stupid reasons. Try to make it work. If you have wealth and are planning to get married, always have a good prenup agreement set up before the wedding date. If it is truly not working and you are going to get a divorce, offer a fair and good settlement to your partner. If they are angry and only want to fight, tell your attorney to stop negotiating and get you in front of a judge. They will usually give you a fair settlement.

My wife, Nancy, and I were married in 1969. We have 5 children and 14 grandchildren. We have had our ups and downs, but we are very supportive of each other. And if she has a problem that I know I can fix immediately, I listen intently and never offer advice. (There is a great and funny YouTube clip by Jason Headly, called "It's Not About the Nail" that makes this point very clear.)

One last comment: I would never be in a relationship that is toxic or does not add true meaning to my life. Sadly, this toxicity could be from parents who are always judgmental and critical of you. Tell any toxic person that, if they continue to be judgmental or critical, you will not be seeing them. I give you permission to take care of yourself first, or else you will not be good to anyone else. Think about what you are teaching your children about the type of relationship they should be in.

LEARNING AND UNDERSTANDING MEDITATION

Meditation helps reduce your stress, increase your energy, clear your brain and relax your body for a deeper, more restful sleep. It makes you feel more connected and less anxious; meditation helps you to be calmer and more clear-headed in demanding situations. It can help you experience better relationships and sharpen your life focus. To learn a simple and powerful form of meditation, I recommend a new book by Emily Fletcher entitled, *Stress Less, Accomplish More: Meditation for Extraordinary Performance.* For a better understanding of the Zeva Technique of meditation, check out her website: https://zivameditation.com/online/ or watch her YouTube video https://www.youtube.com/watch?v=yy6uOoMzbPg.

CREATING LOVE IN YOUR LIFE

Love is that special feeling we get when we have a connection with people and things in our life. It is created when we initiate and give love to people and things. Somebody could love us, and yet we may not feel anything. But we always feel love when we are loving others. I am fortunate to be in a profession where we can love our patients, our team, what we do and especially, our family. This doesn't apply only to loving people but also to things in our lives such as a good movie, a book, a special mug, and other things we go back to and create that feeling of love. Like the movie, *Love Actually*, is all around us.

LETTING GO OF ISSUES AND EMOTIONAL PAIN FROM YOUR PAST

When I was three years old, my mother divorced my father, and he moved to another city. My mother had to go back to school to get her degree, and my brothers and I lived with my grandmother for the next five years. At that young age, I subconsciously blamed myself for their divorce, because if I could have been a better little boy, this would not have happened. I carried this shame and pain through adulthood, hoping that no one would find out how bad I was. I subconsciously stuffed this emotional pain and started to feel from my brain, not my heart, where there was no pain. This inability to feel deep emotions affected many in my personal and business relationships.

I can easily understand why many men are not emotional. Once I addressed the issue and let go of this emotional pain, which can be easily done with proper techniques, my life and I became more emotionally alive and peaceful. Many people carry deeply embedded emotional pain from their past that affects and controls their lives. This could be from abandonment (divorce), which I experienced, sexual abuse, not being wanted—there are many more. One group I work with who are exceptionally good in helping individuals to identify, address and let go of these issues is Legacy Life Consulting. Contact them at: https://www.legacylifeconsulting.com/ David Stamation (208) 946-3894.

YOU NEED TO TAKE CARE OF YOURSELF FIRST

Many people feel they are serving others by giving away all their time and energies helping others, but by doing so, they are not taking care of themselves, leaving them feeling exhausted, frustrated and angry. This is especially true with women. The sad part is, they could better serve and help others if they took care of their own needs first. They need to set time aside just for themselves to love and nurture themselves first; they will feel much better, less resentful and happier as they serve others. The magic word that they need to use more often is "No—I cannot do that. Thanks for asking."

TEACHING YOUR CHILDREN ABOUT LOVING LIFE AND FINANCES

Mahatma Gandhi was asked what his message to the world was. He said, "My life is my message." Teach your children the satisfaction of being a saver instead of a spender. You need to show them the satisfaction of accomplishment and doing a job well. Be the example for them of how they can find fun and joy in everything they do, instead of teaching them duty, responsibility and that you must work hard for a living.

Teach your children to understand the ideas in this book. Help your children find a job, so that they learn to love work, save and be disciplined with their money. Show them the power of getting out of debt and creating and funding their own Roth IRA. Teach them the value of money and the feeling of freedom associated with being debt-free.

STOP COMPLAINING

Half of the people think you deserve what you get, and the other half don't care. My mentor, Kendrick Mercer, shared a story with me after his three-month sailing from California to Lahaina, Maui. His trip was an incredible adventure, with beautiful sunny days, stormy weather, moonbows at night and wonderful solitude. After arriving in Lahaina, he took a plane to Honolulu. He was enjoying the view over the ocean while a lady sitting next to him was complaining to him about her life, children and husband.

During the break in her conversation, he looked at her and said, "Let's play a game. Let's pretend the plane breaks right in half, and we are all going to die. All you see in front of you is the blue sky. We have two choices: we can grab on to the armrest in terror and think about all the things we didn't do in our life, or we can calmly unbuckle our seatbelts, stand up, jump forward, and fly for the rest of our lives." She did not say much after that but gave him a big hug at the end of the flight. Why not live our life in gratitude and enjoy every moment?

LET GO OF ALL ANGER

There are times when others do things to us that make us angry. This is often true in divorce. Sometimes we hold anger, thinking that if we do, it will prevent those things from happening to us again. This prevents us from finding true happiness in the future. **As Buddha said: "Holding onto anger is like drinking poison and expecting the other person to die"**

How Do We Define Success?

This can be different for each one of us. For me, it is about loving what I do each day, being at peace in my life, being in good health, having time to be with and enjoy the people I love, being debt-free, having enough money that I don't worry about money anymore, and having the time and resources to make a difference in the world around me.

Others may define success as being the best businessman, making a lot of money, having time to do missionary work, retiring at age fifty-five, having $2 million in the bank—the list goes on. This book is not meant to define your success but to show you how to have enough time and money to make choices in your life that are right for you. It is not about making a living. It is about making a life worth living.

French writer François-René de Chateaubriand (1768 to 1848) said, "A master in the art of living draws no sharp distinction between his work and his play; his labor and his leisure; his mind and his body; his education and his recreation. He hardly knows which is which; he simply pursues his vision of excellence through whatever he is doing and leaves others to determine whether he is working or playing. To himself, he always appears to be doing both."

HOW MUCH IS ENOUGH?

If you are like most people in the world, one bowl of rice a day would be enough. Here in America, we think in terms of economic freedom. In my past book *Time and Money*, I define "economic freedom" as the day you have accumulated enough safe, liquid assets that can reproduce your lifestyle income (the amount of money it takes to maintain your lifestyle), with safeguards against inflation, for the rest of your life, without touching the principal. This will vary by individual, but once you are debt-free, you could reach that point in five to seven years, simply by following the recommendations in this book.

GET RID OF THE JUNK IN YOUR LIFE

"Junk" is described as anything that does not add meaning to your life right now and drains your energy. There are four types of junk: material junk, time junk, personal junk and conceptual junk. **Material junk** is the exercise machine you walk by every day and never use but makes you feel guilty. It could be all those old clothes in your closet that you never wear and could be donated to someone that could use them. **Time junk** is spending time on things that do not add meaning to your life. You must learn to say "No" to those time wasters that will suck your life away. **Personal junk** are those relationships that drain you and do not add meaning to your life. Focus on those people whom you enjoy being with and who support you on your path. There are two types of **Conceptual junk.** All those things you worry about that you should have done in the past and all those things that you worry about that might happen in the future. We can only live in the moment—the rest is just junk. Stop thinking about the past junk or the future junk, and move your thoughts to those things that you are grateful for in your life now.

DON'T GO DOWN THE RABBIT HOLE

We have between 12,000 and 60,000 thoughts per day, and more than 80% are negative; 95% are repetitive. We have no control over the thoughts that come into our mind, but once they are there, we can dismiss them!!! Focus on gratitude and positive thoughts. Mark Twain said, "I've had many worries in my life, most of which had never happened."

CHARITABLE GIVING

There is a difference between success and significance. One of the great advantages of having more time and more money is the ability to make a difference in the lives of people in the world around us. Charitable giving always brings even more abundance into our life. Even though you are working on paying off debt, donate either your time or money to an important cause. This will make a difference in your life and in the lives of those you help.

THE $2 FREEDOM AND HAPPINESS BILL

I love giving out two-dollar bills as a reminder of our freedom in the United States. This $2 bill is the only piece of US currency that depicts the same person on the front and standing on the back. On the front of the bill, we see Thomas Jefferson, the third president of the United States. Then we turn the bill over and see the signing of the Declaration of Independence. The people standing around the table are the committee who wrote the Declaration. The main author is Thomas Jefferson (the tall person in the center). The person standing on the far left is John Adams, the second president of the United States.

John Adams and Thomas Jefferson had a few things in common: They were both presidents and were the only presidents who signed the Declaration of Independence. They both died on July 4, 1826, within three hours of each other, exactly fifty years after they signed the Declaration of Independence.

In those days, the average man lived to age thirty-five. Adams was ninety, and Jefferson was eighty-three on the day they died. I believe the reason they lived two to three generations beyond the average man is that they were both highly motivated to instill and imprint the ideals of freedom and independence into our American culture. They lived with a purpose.

This is what makes the United States one of the freest countries in the world; we can work and live anywhere we want in this country. We are free to be in any mutual relationship that works, and we are free to leave ones that are toxic (a relationship where you will never grow and are always being put down).

Sadly, most Americans don't know they are free. Many feel trapped in their lives, business, jobs and relationships. They feel angry, controlled, frustrated, anxious or sad. These feelings come from a place of fear—many people fear change and have one foot in and one foot out of their choices (relationships or jobs). These feelings immediately disappear when the person acts, after choosing to change, or by putting "both feet in or out" of their choice.

The $2 bill reminds us of our choice to be free, independent and happy. The secret of happiness is in three choices. Any time you feel upset, angry or trapped, there is something in your life that you are not accepting. The courage to make one of these three choices will give you back your freedom and peace of mind. The choices are as follows:

1. You can change your situation (relationship or work), which takes courage, as you face and conquer your fears. For example, if someone is always judgmental or critical of you and this is a deal-breaker, then you can tell them that behavior is no longer acceptable to you and that, if they continue, you will leave the relationship. If they stop this unacceptable behavior, then you will stay and be at peace. If not, you choose number two.

2. You can leave the situation (relationship or work).

3. If you can't change the situation or choose not to leave the situation, then you can stay and accept the "what is" of the situation and be totally at peace with the situation. Remember that you are the only one that is making you upset. This is an easy choice. You can totally be at peace in your life because all you have to do is change your mind. We need to

change the wording from: "Why is this happening to me?" to "Why is this happening *for* me?"

LEARN TO LOVE YOUR LIFE NOW

Kendrick Mercer had a 50-year-old client from North Carolina. He told him that he'd hated dentistry for the past 25 years and that the worst problem was that he could not quit because he owed so much money. Mercer told him that he could set up his finances so he would be economically free in ten years. Mercer knew the problem was deeper than finances, so he asked him, "Once you reach economic freedom, what are you going to do?"

He said, "I would first quit practicing.

"Then what are you going to do?"

He said, "I am going to play golf."

"Then what are you going to do?"

He said, "I will buy a place on the beach and walk the beach."

"Great—then what are you going to do?"

He said, "And then I will watch TV and read books."

"Then what are you going to do?"

He got really sad and somber, and said, "I will just walk on the beach some more."

"Great—what are you going to do then?"

He started to cry and said, "I'm going to die."

This is a pretty sad story—there there is no aliveness. What he was trying to do was to get someplace instead of loving his life. He would be miserable for ten years in order to get financial freedom. I told him my job was to assist him in knowing that life is never going to be any better or worse than is right now—it's just how you are looking at it. For him to go back and spend one day losing his life for some future time that does not sound that exciting would make his life a failure. He really did not like to hear this, but he knew it was true.

Kendrick told him to go home and promise that he would change his mind and outlook so that he could enjoy dentistry and again appreciate his patients, staff and all relationships. And if he did this and still did not enjoy dentistry, then he would quit, sell everything, and do something in life that he enjoyed. He did go back and began to enjoy his practice. Kendrick continues to coach him and help him create the practice that he loved, with only the right patients, the right team members, and doing the dentistry he loved. Once he slowed down and got out of debt, he started to relax and found renewed life in dentistry. Life is in the present—and because it will never get any better or worse than it is in this minute—it is how we look at our experiences that will make a difference in our lives.

Final Thoughts

LET A PRACTICE-MANAGEMENT COACH help you create the practice you love with efficient systems to become much more profitable. With this extra profit, you can work less *and* eliminate debt quickly while creating investments on your own that will provide the ever-increasing source of passive income described in this book. Many business owners I coach complain about the people they work with who make them miserable. I tell them to go back to their office and tell the owner to fire those people. Then I remind them that *they* are the owner. Most people forget that they can make their business exactly what they want it to be. They have the canvas and the brush.

Stop listening to the news and worrying about what's happening in the stock market or the country. This is just noise. That's it. Now, enjoy your life, grateful for your family and the gifts you have. Spend your money on things that add meaning to your life. This leads to financial freedom and a life of self-integrity and peace.

Economic peace of mind is more than just financial freedom. In fact, we can experience economic peace of mind long before we reach financial freedom. Once we have a solid plan in place for achieving financial freedom, we can let go of our anxiety about money and live as if it has already happened. With this newfound peace of mind, we can truly enjoy life in the moment, because we are secure in what we have, and we know that we can deal with any life challenge.

Once we have a vision and a beautiful story for our lives, we can face life with joy and excitement. With this book, each of us can claim *both* financial freedom *and* economic and personal peace of mind. "Being happy is a choice."

Appendix A

Step-by-Step Debt-Reduction Plan

TO COME UP WITH AN EFFECTIVE STRATEGY for eliminating debt, it's important to have a clear sense of your monthly expenses and to determine how many of these expenses are payments on specific debts. Personal-finance software programs such as Mint.com or Microsoft Money can help you greatly in organizing this information on your computer.

First, write down all debts that you owe, along with the minimum payment for each debt, from the smallest to the largest (see below). We start with the smallest debt because we want to see results quickly, which helps us to continue the plan. Take 10% to 20% of what you make, and set up automatic payment through your bank, starting with the smallest debt. Once that's paid off, move on to the next debt. Continue this until all debt is paid off. You can write a check each month for the extra payment, but automatic payments are much more effective. Very important: All payments must be directed to the principal of the loan, not just to the loan. You will find an in-depth, step-by-step plan below.

Save unexpected extra money, tax returns, bonuses and pay raises, and immediately use this "found money" to pay off your consumer debt. Look for areas in your expenses that you can reduce. Don't buy new cars. You can save thousands of dollars by buying a pre-owned car that is two to five years old. You may want to consider taking a second job for a brief period of time to help eliminate credit-card debt. Some couples live on one salary and pay off debt with the other. Quality of life is found in our relationships, the experience and the detail—not in the number of possessions we own. We need less to live on when we move from a materialistic life to one that is more inspirational and spiritual.

Act Today. Declaring that you are seriously committed to getting out of debt is the first step to achieving personal wealth. Go through the steps below. All forms can be downloaded from https://doctorace.com/resources/ . Also check out the resource section for the debt-free millionaire program and the Smart wealth system.

1. **Sit down with your significant other:** Both of you must be on-board, knowing that this will strengthen your relationship, eliminate stress around money, and give you back your freedom. Then read this book together, and set time aside to do the following:
2. **Add up your net worth,** that is, everything you own, and then subtract everything you owe in the chart below.

Determine Your Net Worth			
Assets	**Amount**	**Liabilities**	**Amount**
Personal Cash (Bank)			
Business Cash (Bank)			
Taxable investments (stocks)			
Tax-deferred investments (IRA/401[k])			
Cash value life insurance			
Gold/Silver			
Other			
Real estate		How much is owed	
Main home		How much is owed	
Vacation homes		How much is owed	
Rental property		How much is owed	
Business building		How much is owed	
Business value		How much is owed	
Other assets		How much is owed	
Automobiles/boat		How much is owed	
Personal property		How much is owed	
Pension (value = 20x yearly amt)		School loans	
Social Security (value = 20x yearly amount)		Credit-card debt	
		Other debt	
Total assets $		Total liabilities $	
		Net worth $ (assets minus liabilities)	

3. Write down your total household income.

Net income source (after taxes)	**Earner A**	**Earner B**
Salary (net, take-home pay)		
Part-time or self-employment income		
Home-based business income		
Investment income		
Social Security		
Pension		
Veteran's benefits		
Other		
Individual totals		
Total income of A and B		

4. Reduce your monthly expenses. List all your current monthly expenses in the "current" column below. In the "reduced" column, record the lowest amount you can reasonably spend on each item. Total up all "reduced" amounts at the bottom of column 3, and then subtract that amount from your total income. The resulting number is your maximum possible *found debt-reduction money.* Go through your credit card receipts and checkbook, and add up all your monthly expenses. Use the list below. See where you can eliminate or reduce certain expenses. Those in bold letters are some of the best places to look for found money.

Monthly expenses	**Current**	**Reduced**
Retirement-plan contributions		
Going out for lunch at work		
Dining out (other than work lunches)		
Groceries (use coupons)		
Telephone (including cell phone)		
Heating fuel		
Water/sewer		
Electricity		
Car cost (fuel and maintenance)		
Parking, tolls, etc. (carpool or bus)		
Car #1 payment		
Car #2 payment		
Insurance—automobile (higher deductibles)		
Insurance—health (higher deductibles)		
Insurance—home (umbrella insurance)		
Insurance—other		
Home-equity loan payment		
Refinance home mortgage (walk away)		
Other loan payment		
Child care		
Cable or satellite TV		
Movies		

Monthly expenses	**Current**	**Reduced**
Streaming Services		
Other entertainment		
Sports (golf, fishing, etc.)		
Health club		
Lawn maintenance		
Laundry and dry cleaning		
Pet food and care		
Subscriptions		
Online computer services		
Credit-card payment		
Credit-card payment		
Credit-card payment		
Christmas gifts		
College education for children		
Private schools		
Emergency fund		
Other savings		
Total reduced monthly expenses =		

Total income minus reduced monthly expenses =

____

(This is your *found debt-reduction money,* which you can use to accelerate your debt payments)

5. **Develop a spending journal,** and, for a month, write down each purchase you make (except regularly scheduled bills). This includes incidentals such as coffee, parking and other items less than a dollar. Use mint.com or download from https://doctorace.com/resources/

Date	Item Purchased	Cash	Credit	Check	Amount

6. **Your Debt-elimination Worksheet** (described below) to pay off all debts within seven to ten years. Read through the debt-elimination-approach description, and then fill out the debt form to see how long it will take you to pay off all debts by making a 10% or 20% payment toward debt each month. I am not a big fan of budgeting. If you are serious about getting out of debt, automatically take 10% or 20% out of your bank account each month as if it were a tax. Live on the rest. **Automation of the payments is the secret!** Filling out the form below will help you understand your financial goals.

Debt-Elimination Worksheet

IDENTIFY YOUR DEBTS, and record them on the Debt-Elimination Worksheet below (you can go to https://doctorace.com/resources/ and download the worksheet). First, pay all small debts (less than $10,000), starting with the smallest. This "small debt" category includes credit-card debt, consumer debt, auto-loan balances and small student loans. Start with the smallest debt (no matter how high or low the interest), and then use the money from your *debt-reduction savings account* to pay it off first, while continuing to make the minimum payments on your other debts.

At the beginning, it's important to get momentum and see that you are making progress, so don't worry about the respective interest rates now. If the high credit-card interest rate on a larger debt bothers you, you can always call the company and successfully negotiate a lower rate or transfer your balance to another credit-card company with a lower rate.

Once you have paid off the first debt, you'll feel a sense of empowerment. Paying off that debt frees up additional money, which you add to your savings. Use this increased savings to pay down the next-smallest debt. Fill out the worksheet in pencil so that you can update it each month. This will help you keep on track and stay motivated.

As you pay down debt, you gain momentum and free up more money to pay off the next debt. The money that pays off these debts comes from increased income, reduced spending, and the extra money that becomes available as you pay off each debt. If you have money saved when you begin setting in motion *Dr. Ace's Financial Freedom Guide*, for the sake of your peace of mind, do *not* use that money for early debt reduction for at least six months. Below is an example of how we pay off debt.

First, determine what percentage of income you want to pay toward debt. If you and your spouse's average income is $72,000, you would divide this by 12 months, giving you $6,000; after taxes, that would be $5,000. 10% of this would be $500 per month.

The $500 (10%) will be paid each month to the principal of the top loan in the chart. First, add the $500 to the VISA Card $30 payment, giving you $530 per month to pay toward that loan, which will be paid off in two months. When the VISA Card is paid off, apply that $530 plus $32 to the next MasterCard loan, which will result in $562; it will take three months to pay off *that* loan. Your efforts will continue to eliminate all your debt. The debts will be paid off in seven years and four months, and you will have an extra $31,176 per year to invest, save, take vacations, send children through college, or work less.

$500 (10%) Paid Monthly to the Principal of Top Loan in the Chart

Name of Debt	Total Balance (smallest to largest)	Monthly Payment	Accelerated Monthly Payment	Months to Pay Off
VISA Card	$1,000	$30	$530	2
MasterCard	$1,500	$32	$562	3
Department store	$2,000	$36	$598	4
Car 1	$9,200	$520	$1,118	9
Car 2	$14,300	$750	$1,868	8
Home-equity loan	$26,000	$370	$2,238	12
Mortgage at 4.5%	$155,000	$860	$3,098	50
Totals	$209,000	$2,598 ($31,176/yr.)		88 months (7 yrs. 4 mo.)

$1,000 (20%) Paid Monthly to the Principal of Top Loan in the Chart

Name of Debt	Total Balance (smallest to largest)	Monthly Payment	Accelerated Monthly Payment	Months to Pay Off
VISA Card	$1,000	$30	$1,030	1
MasterCard	$1,500	$32	$1,062	2
Department store	$2,000	$36	$1,098	2
Car 1	$9,200	$520	$1,618	6
Car 2	$14,300	$750	$2,368	6
Home-equity loan	$26,000	$370	$2,738	10
Mortgage at 4.5%	$155,000	$860	$3,098	43
Totals	$209,000	$2,598 ($31,176/yr.)		70 months (5 yrs. 7 mo.)

Your Debt-Elimination Worksheet: Calculate Paying Off Your Debt

(Annual household income: $ ________________)

(Average American debt is 2.5 times the annual household income)

1. **Determine your extra monthly payments: $____________**

   Try for 10% or more of your monthly take-home income. If you have only a home mortgage, then you should add 20% to 30% of your monthly take-home income.

2. **Write down each debt in the first column below**, prioritizing each debt from smallest to largest. Do not be concerned about the interest rate.

3. **Using the debt-elimination approach, add your accelerator margin to the smallest debt,** making this new monthly payment. Put this in column 4. To determine when the debt will be paid off, divide this amount into the total balance of that debt by the new monthly payment in column 4, and put the number of months to pay off in column 5.

4. **When this debt is paid off, add what used to be the monthly payment amount to the next-smallest debt** payment, and place that in column 4. Again, divide this amount by your new monthly payment in column 4. Put the number of months to pay off in column 5.

5. **Continue adding each paid-off debt's monthly payment amount to its accelerated**

monthly payment and rolling the total amount to the next debt.

6. **Add up the months in column 5 to determine when all debts will be paid off.**

Name of Debt	Total Balance	Monthly Payment	Accelerated Monthly Payment	Months to Pay Off
1	2	3	4	5
Totals				

Things to keep in mind about your debt-elimination plan:

- Use only minimum payments to maximize the debt-elimination process.

- Use only the principal and interest portion of your mortgage payment (not tax/insurance).
- Interest rates are not a big factor.
- Only non-recurring debts go into your debt-elimination plan.

7. **Write and post your Financial Goals.** "I am taking 10% of my income and paying off my debts. In six months (date), I will use 20% of my income toward an extra payment on my debts. I will pay off all credit-card debt in one year (date), my car in two years (date) and my home in six years (date)." Each month, review and challenge yourself to increase your debt reduction.

8. **Develop a support group of either family or co-workers.** Most families' money issues cause the greatest stress, and most do not understand how debt can keep a person in prison and take two thirds of their income throughout their lifetime. In my office, I created and presented to my team and their spouses a debt-reduction plan, which you will find at https://doctorace.com/resources/. In this program, I showed them how to pay off debt, including their home, within 10 years, thereby freeing up more money to invest in their retirement fund. I also showed them how to invest safely, with little risk and higher returns. Within six years, I have four of my employees completely out of debt, including their home, and the others have a game plan to be debt-free within the next 10 years.

9. **Continue to read books** and listen to audios and watch the videos on debt reduction, including the ones found at https://doctorace.com/resources/

10. **Take Dave Ramsey's Financial Peace University** course to help you in a step-by-step approach to getting out of debt and becoming financially free. Financial Peace University: https://www.ramseysolutions.com/ramseyplus/financial-peace/

11. **Become the teacher.** First set up and start the program yourself. Bring your family and friends together and watch these videos. Pass out the handouts, and help them set up the program for themselves. Share other debt-reduction resources with them. Share this material within your community, and help them regain their freedom.

12. **Celebrate Success.**

    This is *not* a no-spending plan; it is a managed-spending plan. I am not saying you can't spend any money on the things you want . . . But I *do* want you to be aware of the impact that each expenditure has on your ability to build your wealth. Most people can easily spend and live on half the amount they normally spend.

Managing Bumps in the Road

IF YOU HAVE AN EMERGENCY during this time—for example, major car repairs or unexpected medical bills—you can use your paid-off credit card or skip a month or two of debt-reduction, payments and use the cash that would have gone toward debts to cover the emergency. The same is true if you feel you need an inexpensive vacation: skip a month or two of debt reduction, and pay for your vacation with cash. Just be sure to get back on track with your debt-reduction plan as soon as you can. I do *not* believe that you must have an emergency fund for you to start debt reduction. Some consultants recommend three to six months of income, but if you wait for that, it might take you two or three years to start your debt-reduction program. Once you have a paid-off credit card, you *do* have an emergency fund.

Once you've made progress paying down your small debt, be sure to fund your Roth IRA and any pension plan at work up to the limit that the company matches your money. Try to fund all company-matched IRA in a Roth IRA.

As soon as you've paid off all your small debts (less than $10,000), celebrate! Now take the "found money" you have freed up and use it to pay off large debts (more than $10,000), such as your car loan, your home mortgage, and any lines of credit. This may seem like a slow process, but once you've paid off all your debts and are regularly investing in your retirement funds, you'll have a considerable amount of excess money left each month to invest in the investment strategies described later in this book. By following this plan, most people can pay off all their credit-card debt in one year and their car in the second year. By the third year, they are making extra payments toward the principal on their mortgage. Most people following this plan can be debt-free and pay off their home in seven to ten years.

When your last debt (home) is paid off, 40% to 60% of your income will be available for investments or to place into your savings. This will allow you to become totally financially free in another eight or nine years. Figures 3 and 4 are examples of the debt-elimination approach to paying off your debts.

Appendix B

Ideas on How to Find and Make More Money

- ✓ https://www.ruleoneinvesting.com/blog/personal-development/ways-to-make-extra-money/
- ✓ An extra job becomes the rocket booster to accelerate your debt reduction.
- ✓ Make more at your job, and put it toward debt.
- ✓ Do consulting work from home.
- ✓ Set up an eBay account and business.
- ✓ Learn how to create an online business at home.
- ✓ Go to clients at their home (bookkeepers or computer experts).
- ✓ Teach college at night.
- ✓ Check out Internet on "work-at-home jobs" (beware of scams).
- ✓ Multilevel marketing (e.g., Mary Kay) (beware of scams).

- ✓ Go back to school to give you opportunities for a higher-paying job, and make all efforts to limit your student-loan debts.
- ✓ With an extra job, you could be debt-free three years earlier.

OTHER IDEAS FOR FINDING EXTRA MONEY

- ✓ Stop funding retirement until debt-free, except for matching contributions.
- ✓ Get rid of your emergency fund. Once your credit card is paid, it becomes your emergency fund.
- ✓ Evaluate/reduce holiday gift giving.
- ✓ Check bank/credit-card statement.
- ✓ Stop smoking.
- ✓ Properly maintain your home and car.
- ✓ Never buy a brand-new car until debt-free.
- ✓ Never finance beyond 36 months.
- ✓ Take advantage of "cheap," meaningful vacations.
- ✓ Don't buy tools/boats you don't often use—rent or borrow them.
- ✓ Conserve utility usage.
- ✓ Avoid "Retail Therapy."
- ✓ Learn to say "No" to kids.
- ✓ Think like Warren Buffet, and send your children to public grade schools and high schools instead of private schools.

- ✓ Stop funding your children's education. Let them pay for college and apply for as many scholarships as they can. Many scholarships never get applied for.
- ✓ Apply all bonuses and pay raises toward debt.
- ✓ Eliminate private mortgage insurance (PMI) by paying down the mortgage balance to 80% of the home's original appraised value.
- ✓ Evaluate your real insurance needs.
- ✓ Auto insurance: get higher deductibles.
- ✓ Personal-liability insurance.
- ✓ Medical insurance.
- ✓ Get higher deductibles.
- ✓ Get an umbrella attachment.
- ✓ Never buy extended warranties.
- ✓ Use coupons (retailmenot.com, Joinhoney.com).
- ✓ Stop getting tax refunds.
- ✓ Spare-change jar.
- ✓ Have only a cell phone.
- ✓ Minimize dining out. Move to brown-bag lunches.
- ✓ Simplified lifestyle.
- ✓ Entertainment—Movies—Get rid of cable, satellite TV and streaming services.
- ✓ Shop at outlet malls/Goodwill.

- ✓ See if you can refinance your home at a lower rate without fees through Quicken loans or a local bank.
- ✓ Buy a duplex, and live on one side; use your renter payment to double your monthly mortgage payments. Look at prebuilt homes as a starter home.
- ✓ One of the fastest ways to become debt-free is to move to a cheaper location. The average home price in the US is $348,500 in 2024. It is a lot easier to get out of debt if you buy your home in a location where the home prices are low, such as in West Virginia for $143,200, Indiana and Ohio at $180,000, compared to San Jose, California, where the average home is $1,406,957.

This is *not* a no-spending plan; it is a managed-spending plan. I am not saying you can't spend any money on the things you want. But I *do* want you to be aware of the impact that each expenditure has on your ability to build your wealth. Most people can easily spend and live on half the amount they normally spend.

Appendix C

Learning to Invest on Your Own

Rule One Investing

I'M ABOUT TO SHARE WITH YOU an easy-to-learn, effective investment strategy. It is not that complicated, and once you learn it, you will need to spend only an hour a month working on your investment portfolio. This is much better than entrusting your funds to a financial adviser or fund manager who might end up taking 75% of the money you have earned. Yes, initially it requires some time and action, but what I'll guide you through is so straightforward that anyone, even those with no prior investment experience or with an aversion to math, can manage it. Using this approach, you could obtain an annual return of 15%, which would be double the 7% average market return.

To make this happen for yourself, you need to understand the rules. Every successful investor, whether actively trading or a long-term investor, abides by Warren Buffet's two rules: rule #1—Don't lose money, and rule #2—Don't forget rule #1.

The embodiment of this philosophy can be found in the books written by Phil Town entitled: *Rule #1, Payback Time*, and *Invested*—all national bestsellers. In these books, he helps you find wonderful companies using technical tools to help you determine the true valuation of a company. This will help you purchase these companies at the best time and the best price. This will be discussed in this chapter. If you truly want to learn and understand how to invest on your own, then check out his website at: https://www.ruleoneinvesting.com/

To retire financially independent, you must learn to grow your retirement funds on your own. This will also give you the extra funds needed to enjoy your life before you eventually step away from the workforce. Investing safely and predictably in the stock market is the fastest way to grow wealth through compound interest.

Albert Einstein once said: "Compound interest is the eighth wonder of the world. He who understands it, earns it . . . he who doesn't, pays it." Here is a real-life example.

When I was at Command and General Staff College back in 1981, the post commander, LT General Howard Stone, spoke to the entire school one afternoon on finances. He told us to pay attention to where we spend our money and to put 10% to 15% toward debt reduction and savings. The saved money should be put into an IRA. This will teach us the power of compound interest.

At that time, the maximum you could put in was $2,000, so I took $4,000 and funded my IRA for 1981 and 1982 with a broker at Edward Jones. He put me into a good loaded mutual fund that, fortunately, gave the same return as the S&P 500 index fund. That was the only time I ever invested in the market until the year 2000. General Stone wasn't around, so I never looked at or worried about that investment for 18 years.

In January 2000, I was shocked to see that my $4,000 had grown to $105,000, an overall return of twenty-six times. This is when I began to understand the power of compound interest and the importance of just staying in the market. At a 15% annual return, that $105,000 could have grown from 2000 to 2024 to more than **$3.76 million** over 42 years. **Remember that this was a one-time investment of only $4,000.**

If that money had been invested in a Roth IRA with a 3% dividend yield, I would be getting more than $110,000 tax free that year. Over the next 8 years, with a 10% dividend-growth rate and a 15% annual return, my yearly tax-free income could be $450,000, and the portfolio would be worth $12.8 million. Just think how many millions of dollars I would have had if I had put in the maximum to my IRA account each year from 1982 and understood how to invest it safely on my own.

Many individuals get confused with investing and do not understand how easy it is to invest on their own through a company like Charles Schwab. That is why they are so vulnerable to dangerous investment schemes, high-fee advisers and brokers that will destroy any chance for them to have a comfortable retirement.

Learning to invest on your own and creating generational wealth is not complicated! The secret to becoming financially free is to first make more money in your office and quickly pay off debt. During this time, you can learn how to trade in the stock market using risk-free paper trading as described below. Also learn how to maximize your personal investments in a tax-free environment such as a Roth 401(k) safe-harbor profit-sharing plan, which will be described below.

These options are never offered to you by your financial advisers because no one makes money from them. What you are offered are risky stocks and mutual funds with low returns, high commissions, and adviser fees, along with the high anxiety associated with these products. The other supposedly safe type of investment are low-return bonds or treasuries that will never provide adequate passive income for your life.

HOW TO START

The idea of investing on your own and understanding stocks and the stock market can seem overwhelming. It is not that hard once you learn a simple and systematic approach to picking great companies and buying them when they are on sale. By learning to invest now, you will be able to create a constant source of increasing passive income for you and your family over your lifetime. This chapter gives you an insight and overview of the investing process.

Over the long run, investing in the stock market produces the best returns of any investment. It is better than bonds, better than gold, and even better than real estate, if you do it the right way. When you buy stocks, you benefit in two ways: from any increases in the price of shares and from any dividends that the company pays to you as an investor.

To learn how to invest in the stock market and get the best returns, you will need a great teacher. I am not that teacher. But I can introduce you to my mentor, Phil Town, the founder of Rule One Investing. He will help and coach you through this process. He believes that, with the proper one-on-one personal training, you could average more than 15% annual return on your investments in the stock market. I have found this to be true for me, and I get no compensation for sharing this information.

You do not have to be a genius to invest when you understand Rule One. It was created for the ordinary person just like you. Many people think you must take high risk to get high rewards in investing. This is just the opposite of Rule One investing. Here you can get high returns of 15% with low risk and reach retirement and financial independence a lot sooner.

You will find much valuable information on his website, his books, and through his three-day virtual webinar. You are not going to learn how to best invest from this book or from any other book any more than you can learn to fly a plane by reading about flying in a book. You must go fly the plane and get the feel of it for real. To accelerate your learning experiences without making fateful mistakes, learn paper trading. This is taught in his hands-on Zoom course. Here you will learn a step-by-step approach on how to invest like Warren Buffett for only $97. These three days are your first step to financial freedom.

https://www.ruleoneinvesting.com/virtual-investing-workshop/.

This Zoom course is the best I have ever taken to learn how to invest on my own without risk through paper trading. It is personally taught by Phil Town himself, along with his great instructors. In my small Zoom group of 8 students, we had 2 instructors to handhold us through each process and showed us how to find great companies and buy them at half price.

Also check out his website and his blogs on learning to invest, financial control, stock basics, investment news and tips, retirement planning, and personal development.

https://www.ruleoneinvesting.com/blog/stock-market-basics /become-investor/

https://www.ruleoneinvesting.com/blog/stock-market-basics/how -the-market-works/

https://www.ruleoneinvesting.com/blog/how-to-invest/value -investing/

You first need to set up an account in a brokerage house that has a great trading platform and the tools and indicators to help you understand when the best time is to get in or to get out of the market. I recommend Charles Schwab. I have no connection with

Charles Schwab, other than I like and use their services. They have low or no fees for trading stocks, a user-friendly interface, an easy-to-understand trading platform and incredible customer service.

It is an American multinational financial-services company. It offers banking, commercial banking, an electronic trading platform and wealth-management adviser services to both retail and institutional clients. It has more than 360 branches, primarily in financial centers in the United States and the United Kingdom. It is the 13th-largest banking institution in the United States, with more than $6.6 trillion in client assets. It is one of the three largest asset managers in the world.

Charles Schwab is open 24 hours a day, 7 days a week, and has excellent representatives and brokers. Schwab has no dollar minimums to open an account. It has one of the lowest expense ratios for the S&P 500 funds. When you purchase stocks and index ETFs (exchange-traded funds), there are no trading fees or commissions.

While Schwab was designed to sell stocks and provide stock investors with the most current research and other useful information, they offer everything that any big bank would offer, including checking and savings accounts.

All representatives and Schwab brokers are salaried; they do not work on commission, so their advice focuses on your best interests. Schwab has agents located in most large cities. These local Schwab brokers can help you open an account, but it may be easier to go online and have an account set up within 30 minutes. You can call their online representative (800-435-4000) to help you through this process. Set up your Charles Schwab account:

https://www.schwab.com/client-home

Once you set up an account, you'll then need to "fund" your Charles Schwab cash account (not margin account) by linking it to your personal bank accounts. Call up a Schwab representative to help you create this link. Within a day, you will be able to transfer money from your own bank account into your Schwab investment account. Once it is set up, then transfer the amount of money you plan to invest. You can also set up an automatic transfer each month if you would like. Initially, there is no money needed to open an account.

Another option is to just send a check to Schwab. Check with a representative to verify the correct address to send the check to, and write your name and account number on the check. After your brokerage account is set up, download the Charles Schwab app onto your phone.

They recently acquired Ameritrade and their trading platform, called *thinkorswim*. This is one of the best platforms to help you practice trading in the stock market without risk, using paper trades. Not only is it a great platform for determining when to buy in and get out of stocks but also for those who are interested in option trading. Ask your Schwab representative how to download and use *thinkorswim*. Check out the YouTube videos on how to use *thinkorswim*. This is your golden ticket to becoming a successful investor.

https://www.youtube.com/watch?v=W5gJ5-p-8O8&list=PL5F91D714FC3CDE21&index=1

UNDERSTANDING RULE ONE INVESTING

This system is not that hard to learn. My 12-year-old grandson is using what he learned in this course to invest in his Roth IRA. This is how you teach and create generational wealth. Of the many different investing strategies that a modern-day investor may choose, value investing is the best. It is also the foundation of the Rule One investing strategy. Once you learn this system, you will need to spend only 15 minutes a week doing option trading and following the statistics of the 6 to 15 companies you own or want to own.

Warren Buffett recommends that investors concentrate their investments in a limited number of well-known, high-quality businesses. During a talk at Georgetown University on Sept. 19, 2013, Buffett described the punch-card-strategy approach as follows: *"You have an opinion on only a few things. In fact, I've told students that, if, when they got out of school, they should get a punch card with 20 punches on it, and that's all the investment decisions they got to make in their entire life; they would get very rich because they would think very hard about each one."*

Quite simply, invest as if you had only 20 investing possibilities in your lifetime. For the punch-card approach to work, you find and research wonderful companies that you can purchase at half price. Then invest for the long run. It prevents investors from succumbing to the urge to trade excessively and concentrate on the best companies, resulting in long-term rewards.

Here are the steps to Rule One investing. First, we must find a wonderful company. To help us, we use the Rule One toolbox scanner to create a watch list of wonderful companies and the price you are willing to pay. These are the businesses you want to own and that you will buy if the price is right. Your watch list won't be long. Over time, you may have only 6 to 15 companies that you own. A portfolio of 6 to 15 high-quality income stocks spread out reasonably over different sectors provides a compelling balance between the benefits of diversification and of concentration. One of the best places to find great companies is through the Rule One toolbox search section.

The toolbox will help us determine the true, intrinsic retail value of the company. Next, we calculate the margin-of-safety price of these companies. This is usually 50% of the intrinsic retail value of the company. When the price drops to our margin-of-safety price, which is half of the retail value price, we buy the company. If the price continues to drop, then we will buy more shares as long as it still remains a wonderful company.

When the company grows over time to exceed 20% of the intrinsic retail value, we may want to sell the company. We use this money to buy other undervalued companies or to buy the same company when it is on sale for half price. We continue to do this until we are rich.

Our goal is to have 6 to 15 wonderful companies that we own. While we wait for the margin-of-safety price, we can do option trading. The Rule One Zoom course will teach you how to do option trading with very little risk, with a potential annual return of 20%. This takes only about 15 minutes per week to either see if the company is ready to buy or to put in your option trades.

Value investing is a strategy focusing on buying companies with a low price-to-earnings multiple. Ben Graham, Warren Buffett's mentor, is the father of value investing and wrote the bible of value investing, *Security Analysis* in 1934. This book is still in print today.

He called this "value" investing because, ideally, each investment had more value than was paid in the price. In essence, the idea is to get $10 of value for a $5 price.

By the time Warren Buffett started investing money, though, the economy had changed, and finding deeply undervalued companies was not as easy as it had been in Graham's time. To adapt, Buffett adjusted the theory somewhat, choosing to focus on finding companies that were not only undervalued but were also wonderful businesses with a highly predictable future. Buffett also recommends that you buy only companies that you understand. He calls this your "circle of competence."

Rule One investing dictates that the best way to make large returns on your investments is to find a few intrinsically wonderful companies, run by good people and priced much lower than their actual value. A business that hits all these marks constitutes a Rule One company.

FINDING WONDERFUL COMPANIES

Wonderful companies have products that are universal, have honest management, can raise prices during inflationary times, maintain large profit margins, have little or no debt, and make the world a better place.

USE THE 4-Ms

First you must ensure that the companies you are investing in are high-quality enough to retain their value throughout the time you are holding them. I like to evaluate whether a business is a wonderful company with what I call the 4-Ms of Investing: Meaning, Management, Moat and Margin of Safety. Of the four, the Margin of Safety does not tell you if it is a good company, but it does help you buy these wonderful companies at half price.

Meaning–You must understand the meaning of the business. How does this industry work, who are the competitors, and how do they compete? And how does this business fit your personal values? Does it have meaning to you personally? This is important because, if it has meaning to you, you'll better understand what it does and how it works. You'll be more likely to do the research necessary to understand all elements of the business that affect its value.

Management–The company needs to have management that is talented and has integrity. Perform a background check on the leaders in charge of guiding the company, paying close attention to their honesty, transparency and success of their prior positions to determine if they are good, solid leaders that will take the company in the right direction. And, super-critically: Do they allocate capital well?

Moat—The company should have a moat. A moat is something intrinsic to business, making it very difficult for competitors to compete. If a company has patented technology, a network of users, control over the market, an impenetrable brand or a product or service customers would never switch from, it has a moat. Commodity companies rarely have a moat and are not usually on our watch list.

Margin of Safety—To guarantee good returns, you must buy a company at a price that gives you a margin of safety. For Rule One investors, 50% off the intrinsic value (retail price) is the Margin of Safety to look for. This provides a buffer that makes it possible to still experience gains even if problems arise. This is the final M, but arguably the most important.

These 4-Ms separate Rule One investing from value investing. Both dictate that you must buy a company at a good price, but Rule One strategy requires a much deeper understanding of the business. We reduce risk with knowledge. That's the bottom line.

DETERMINE THE COMPANY'S INTRINSIC VALUE

At its core, a Rule One stock is a company that is priced at half of its intrinsic value (fair market value/retail price). The problem is knowing what the true intrinsic value is. This term is thrown around a lot regarding value investing. The key to your investing success is to buy companies at the margin-of-safety price, which is half of the intrinsic value price. One of the best ways of finding this is to use the Rule One toolbox.

Phil Town, in his books and in his courses, discusses three ways of determining the intrinsic value of a company. These are called the Margin of Safety, payback time and 10 cap. There are different valuation methods for companies, depending on where the company is in its life cycle. Here are the three methodologies.

Margin of Safety involves buying a stock at a price significantly below its intrinsic value. It provides a buffer against errors in estimation and unforeseen adverse events. This method is best used for younger companies who are in higher growth and are putting a lot of their money back into growing the business. A great example of a company where this valuation method would be used is Netflix.

Payback time refers to the estimated time it takes for an investor to recoup their initial investment through the company's future free-cash flows. Investors using the payback-time method want to identify stocks where the expected free-cash flows will allow them to recover their investment within a reasonable time frame. PayPal is an example of a company where we might use this method.

The 10 Cap (capitalization rate) valuation method is a favorite among some investors because it is the easiest to do, and it doesn't depend on coming up with some arbitrary growth rate for the next 10 years, which is just unknowable. All I have to know is: Will this company be bigger and better in 10 years?" This method is great for up-and-coming companies, like Sprouts Farmers Market. We can ask simple questions like: Will there be more stores in 10 years? If the answer is "Yes," we take the annual earnings, multiply by 10, and achieve the valuation.

These calculations require tools and practice to fully know and understand which methodology to use, how to do the calculations, and attach an accurate intrinsic value. This is why they teach this in their three-day virtual Zoom workshops. They are automatically calculated in the toolbox under "research valuation calculator." These are used only as guidelines because you need to do your own research on each of these companies. They also have a graph that shows you the buy price, 20% above the buy price, the sticker price, and 20% above the sticker price. See, below, these evaluations on Ulta Beauty Inc. (ULTA).

Then calculate the sticker price at $663.34 and the buy price at $331.67. The current price is $431.35, which is very close to the buy price. As you can see from the toolbox, ULTA has the highest Rule One score of 99, indicating it is a wonderful company.

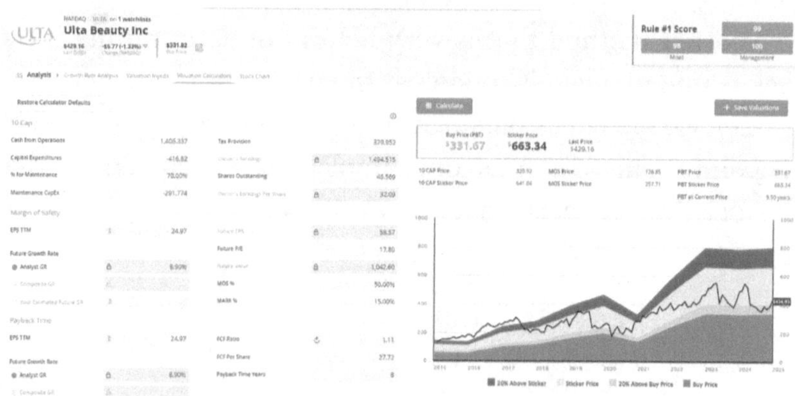

The reason we do all three is to verify that they are telling the same story! It's like a system of checks and balances to make sure we fully understand the business and are able to make an investment that will deliver maximum returns for years to come.

How do you decide when to use these things? Initially, run all three. A lot of companies, particularly with growth rates of 15% to 20%, have valuations very similar. Just add them up, divide them by three, and take the average.

When the growth rates are low, 5% to 8% growth with a low PE ratio, your Margin of Safety valuation is going to be a lot lower than the 10 cap and the payback time. In that case, we don't just add them all together but use the two that are very similar. Occasionally all three of them are all over the map; consider that a red flag, and look for another company.

Another method that is very helpful in determining if the stock is undervalued is to look at the price of the stock over its 52-week range. Focus on stocks that are close to their 52-week low point. Using ULTA as an example, above, you can see that the stock lies very close to its 52-week low.

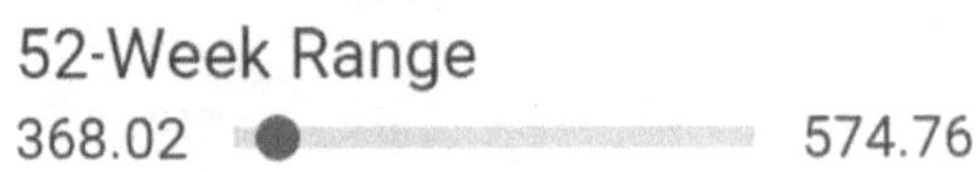

Buying stocks when they are undervalued is one of the most important criteria in stock selection. Our goal is to buy wonderful companies at half the sticker price when they are on sale. Wait until these companies' price ranges are at the lower end of their 52-week low/high range.

Many investors look for companies that are cheap. A Rule One investor knows that it is better to buy a wonderful business at a fair price than a fair business at a wonderful price. Rule One investors require a deep understanding of the companies before they buy. They must know the business well enough and understand that it's wonderful. This mindset is an important step in learning value investing. While it may not appear all that complex, buying $10 bills for $5 can be an emotional challenge, but with the right mindset, most can master it.

Warren Buffett has said that emotions are the enemy of a rational investor. The biggest problem with young investors is overconfidence in believing that they know more than they know. This is called "confirmation bias," where you can no longer see anything negative about the company. All great investors look at inversion. Before they make a decision to buy a company, they look at all the things that can go wrong or what is bad with the company.

Fear is your friend. Buffett said that the secret to great investing results is to buy when there is **Fear! Fear** is what makes the market price of a wonderful business fall substantially lower than its intrinsic value.

Focus on the long term. Buy businesses at the right time, and know that the right time will present itself if you're patient. Everyday stock-market volatility and events such as recessions, market crashes and negative publicity, among others, create opportunities for value investors to jump in and buy when the price drops. We want to see the market go down so that we can buy great companies at a significant discount.

An example of such an event was the E coli scares with Chipotle Mexican Grill (CMG) in 2015, when the stock dropped from $700 a share down to $250 a share in 2018. This was a strong, well-run company that rebounded from a low of $250 a share to $3280 a share on Tuesday, June 25, 2024. It has since had a 50-to-1 stock split as of June 26 to the price of $66 post-stock split.

Finding underpriced wonderful companies does not happen every day. Charlie Munger said we don't make money when we buy, and we don't make money when we sell; **we make money when we wait.** While we wait for wonderful companies to go on sale, we spend very little time on investing while enjoying the fun parts of life. During our free time, we do our research to create a watch list of wonderful companies that we want to buy. For those investors who want to try to maximize their investment assets, they can learn how to trade options safely.

In the 1960s, when Warren Buffett had only a small amount of money to invest, he was able to get annual returns of up to 50% by finding smaller undervalued growth companies with great potential. Over the past 10 years, Buffett's returns have only matched the S&P 500 because of its size and inability to move in and out of the market quickly. Small individual investors like us have a great advantage over large institutional investors. We have the advantage of finding smaller undervalued wonderful companies with great potential that are not on the radar of large investors. Use the toolbox scanner to help find these companies.

Learn to invest with great teachers. Once you have learned, become an independent thinker, and make your own purchase decisions. Try not to rely on other people to give you recommendations.

RESEARCH SOURCES AND WEBSITES

Today we have many great Internet resources to quickly look for and research wonderful companies. The best one I have found is the Rule One toolbox https://www.ruleonetoolbox.com/login. You can sign up for a 14-day free trial. You will also get three months free when you take the $97 three-day Zoom video workshop. The monthly cost is about $30.

Here, you can get information that is hard to get anywhere else. Through their stock scanner, you can filter stocks based on specific parameters. Some of these parameters may be a market cap greater than $300 million, long-term debt less than two years of earnings, return on investment capital (ROIC) of 15% or greater and a Rule One safety score of 85% or greater. You may want to eliminate from your search all companies that are biotech or pharmaceutical, those that are pure technology, those that are banks or insurance companies and any companies from China. These are just examples.

You can search for the important numbers of great companies using the Rule One criteria for calculating growth rates, the moat and management numbers, and pricing and valuations. It has links to the company's annual reports and 10-K's (10-K is short for Form 10-K, which is a document the Securities and Exchange Commission requires all public companies to file each year.) plus a list of what companies the investment gurus are buying or selling. It even color-codes the results so you can easily see which companies to look at and which companies you should avoid. You will learn how to use this toolbox when you take the Rule One virtual three-day course and receive a three-month subscription to the toolbox for free. https://www.youtube.com/watch?v=wmuPCLoo4U8&t=292s

The best resource for investment terminology is https://www.investopedia.com/. Below are the best free investment-research websites that I use to do my research. They also have good stock screeners. You can go on YouTube to see how they work. There are upgrades you can purchase for more in-depth research.

Charles Schwab (free)—https://client.schwab.com/app/research/#/tools/stocks

Seeking Alpha (free)—https://seekingalpha.com/

Yahoo finance (free)—https://finance.yahoo.com/

There are also three YouTube sites that I use in my research. They are:

New money—https://www.youtube.com/@NewMoneyYouTube/videos

Investor center—https://www.youtube.com/@InvestorCenter/videos

Rule 1 investing—https://www.youtube.com/@PhilTownRule1Investing

Red Flags—In chapter 5 of Phil Town's *Payback Time*, he lists six red flags that you need to watch out for when selecting a company. The **first** is that it has no meaning to you. If you're not an expert in an industry, you don't have any business owning a company in that industry. **Second**, it has no moat. If there is no durable competitive advantage, don't even consider it. Without a moat, a business has to compete on price. **Third**, the CEO is a poor leader without vision or strong values.

Fourth, the company cannot pay off its debt within three years. To check this, divide the total long-term debt by current earnings. **Ideally, we would like to see no debt**. **Fifth**, the company has powerful trade unions that can destroy its competitive edge. **Sixth**, be careful of technology companies, as their moat can disappear overnight with new technology.

PAPER TRADING

In the virtual course, you will learn how to set up a *thinkorswim* trading platform and use it to practice with paper money (you get $100,000 in Monopoly-like play money). This will help you overcome the fear of investing and the possibility of losing money while you learn how to invest safely. Once you open a trading account with Charles Schwab, call them; let them help you download the *thinkorswim* platform and show you how to make a paper trade. Set up your *thinkorswim* platform indicators following the YouTube link below:

https://www.youtube.com/watch?v=dr9r9AQL1po

To paper-trade, you start by searching for a business that's wonderful and available at an attractive price. Use the toolbox to help you focus your search. Do the 4-M analysis on businesses until you find one that works for you. In your notebook, write down the name of the business and the symbol, the Sticker Price and the MOS Price. Charles Schwab will usually start you out with $100,000 of fake money to practice with. Review the indicators for the businesses you want to buy, and when you have three indicators that say, "Get in," buy the business on paper.

Open a Charles Schwab account for your children and set up their own *thinkorswim* platform. Teach them to invest in the stock market without fear and enjoy the process of buying and selling stocks using paper money on *thinkorswim*. This will be better than any of the video games they're playing now.

THINKORSWIM INDICATORS, FACs AND TREND LINES

Stocks move up or down, not so much in reaction to events that are happening. Events can and do affect the decision of the institutional fund manager to buy or sell the stocks, but, in the end, the price of the stock goes up or down only because of increased or decreased institutional investing. Because the big guys are more than 80% of the market, it takes them 6 to 12 weeks to get totally in or out of a company. For small investors like us, it takes us only about 10 seconds to do the same.

Since January 2014, Warren Buffett's Berkshire Hathaway and the S&P 500 have had the same annualized rate of return, including reinvestment of dividends of 12%. The reason Buffett is not getting the high returns he had in the past is because he is too big and cannot move in and out of the market as quickly as we can. This allows us to get greater returns than the S&P 500.

Being small gives us a great advantage over these large institutional investors. To help us identify when the big boys are getting in and out, we use tools known as "technical indicators." There are three indicators that are very helpful, and when all of them line up saying "buy," it's time to get in. When all three are saying "sell," it's time to get out. Simple.

Once you have identified a wonderful business that passes all 4-Ms and you can buy it at 50% margin of safety, these indicators help you have the courage to invest in those great companies. These indicators are fantastic at keeping you from losing money if you are buying businesses at prices below their value (the sticker price). The only way to make money with certainty in any kind of investment is to buy it well below its value. Doing that will make you very rich.

The best source is the Charles Schwab 3 indicators found on their trading platform called *thinkorswim*. Once you've downloaded the platform, use the following YouTube link to set up these indicators correctly. https://www.youtube.com/watch?v=dr9r9AQL1p0. These indicators are described in more detail in chapter 12 in Phil Town's book *Rule #1: The Simple Strategy for Getting Rich—in Only 15 Minutes a Week!*

The first indicator is called the moving average. This tool tracks the average price of a stock during a specific time period. Moving averages are simply closing prices over a defined number of days divided by that number of days. There are a lot of technical traders out there who trigger their buying and selling with a moving average. The moving average smooths out the peaks and valleys of daily price fluctuations and gives traders an easy view of the price trend.

Technical traders (which we are not) don't even think about what a business is worth. All they want to know is whether it's going to move up or down, based on these or similar indicators. Technical traders make their buying and selling decisions based solely on price and do not undergo an analysis of the fundamentals of the company. They don't care about anything else except price movements. When the price line crosses above the moving average line, they buy. When the price line crosses below the moving average line, they sell.

The second indicator is the MACD—Moving Average Convergence Divergence. Developed by an economist, Dr. Gerald Appel, the MACD is probably the most consistent indicator of significant trend changes in a stock, and it's certainly the most used technical indicator in the world. It looks at several price-average changes over time, generally in the short term. It shows us when momentum pressure is getting stronger, either upward or downward. Since most of the money in the market is institutional, the MACD shows us when the big guys are sneaking in or sneaking out. The MACD is the combination of two moving averages—a fast one and a slow one—and how they interact.

The third indicator is the slow stochastic, developed by Dr. George C. Lane. This is a momentum tool that tracks the overbuying and overselling of a stock. The stochastic looks at the high price and the low price of a stock over a 14-trading-days period. When the price goes below the 20th percentile, the stock is getting oversold—too many sellers and not enough buyers.

When it moves up through the 20th percentile, it often means the big guys are starting to seriously buy and that the price is likely to go up. When the price moves well above the 80th percentile, the stock is going into an overbought condition—too many buyers and not enough sellers. As it drops below the 80th percentile, it indicates the big guys were seriously taking profits and that the price is likely to drop.

Here is an example of using *thinkorswim* and the three indicators we have discussed set for monthly charting, using T Rowe Price as our example from July 2019 until February 2024. In March 2019, you were able to see the three arrows in the monthly chart going up and get in at $112. In December 2021, you saw the three arrows going down and you would have gotten out at $200. We then wait for the three arrows to go up in May 2023 and buy in at $108. In March 2019 the stochastic had no green arrow, but the line was moving upward, which qualifies as a green arrow.

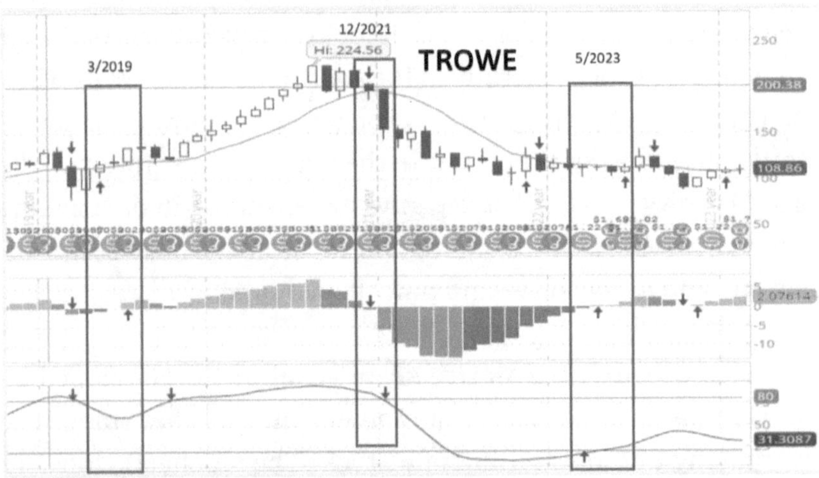

These indicators do help us in our buying decisions, but we first need to do our research to determine if this is a wonderful company to buy. Then focus on the 4-Ms and the true intrinsic value of the company, and buy it at half price. If we ignore the 4-Ms and accidentally buy businesses that are priced above their value, the prices of those businesses will eventually correct themselves downward toward the Sticker Price, and we lose money.

These indicators are very helpful when we're trying to buy businesses below their intrinsic value (the Sticker Price). The only way to make money with certainty in any kind of investment is to buy it well below its intrinsic value.

THE FLOORS AND CEILINGS (FACs)

The Floors and Ceilings (FACs) is a strategy for timing stock purchases based on the recurring patterns in a stock's price movement, utilizing psychological cues known as Floors and Ceilings (FACs). FACs play a crucial role in optimizing the timing of stockpiling, particularly when aiming for substantial discounts to the MOS (Margin of Safety) Price.

As value investors, we wait to buy a great company when it is at or below 50% of its sticker price, which is called "Margin of Safety." At that time, we will stockpile. This is a term used to indicate initially putting a portion of our total capital we want to invest in the business, such as 25%. We then take advantage of the floors and ceilings lines to add another 25% or 50% as the stock drops lower and hits the floor.

FACs are rooted in the understanding that significant market players, such as fund managers controlling substantial sums in the market, tend to fixate on specific price targets. Although psychological in nature, FACs hold tangible significance. For instance, if a fund manager decides to buy a stock at $70 based on historical bounces at that price, it becomes a psychological floor in the price, akin to a solid foundation.

Observing any stock-price chart reveals that prices seldom ascend continuously; periodic reversals are inherent, even in bullish markets. These pullbacks are influenced by the emotions and psyches of investors, particularly the influential Big Guys. These market players may get apprehensive or overly optimistic, prompting them to initiate selling when this perceives a potential peak in the stock's price.

This time-consuming process of exiting positions requires anticipation of a mass exit, leading to selling actions. While selling safeguards against overstaying in the market, it also allows fund managers to realize profits. If the price stops declining after selling begins, fund managers might re-enter the market, starting another upward trajectory. This FACs stockpiling method labels a recurring price level a "Floor," signifying a point where a falling price tends to halt its descent. A Floor is identified when the price consistently rebounds off a specific level without breaking downward; the frequency of these bounces determines the strength of the Floor. Conversely, when the price ceases its ascent and either descends or stabilizes, the FAC method designates this recurring level as a "Ceiling," implying a barrier that the price struggles to surpass.

Notably, when a price finally reaches a Ceiling and moves upward, the former Ceiling often transforms into a new Floor. Stock prices exhibit a somewhat consistent pattern of movement between Floors and Ceilings before breaking through or possibly retracing to test the previous Ceiling as a new Floor.

On a price chart depicting a business's stock-price evolution, Floors and Ceilings are visualized as horizontal lines representing points where the price halts and reverses direction, shaped by recurrent reversals at specific price levels.

An additional element to consider is the Trend lines, depicted diagonally on the chart; these serve as imaginary boundaries that form a Resistance at the top and a Support at the bottom. Trend lines are imaginary diagonal lines that form over a long time. Floor and Ceiling lines are imaginary horizontal lines that form over a short time.

While distinct from Floors and Ceilings, Trend lines are used similarly to predict potential price reversals, offering an additional layer of analysis for strategic decision-making. You can draw these Floor and Ceiling lines as well as Trend lines using the drawing tools on your *thinkorswim* platform, as you see below.

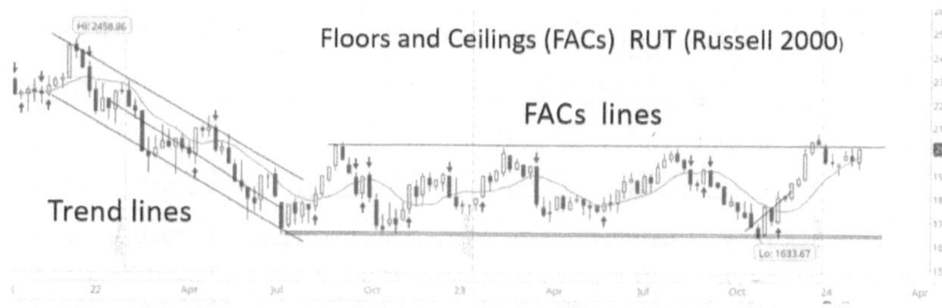

Fibonacci Retracements help us see Floors and Ceilings (FACs) that may not be obvious at first glance. You can create Fibonacci retracements in *thinkorswim* by drawing lines between the high and low time. Generally, use a six-to-nine-month time frame day chart, and try to look for the best fit. See example below.

To learn more, read chapter 6 in Phil Town's *Payback Time.* You will learn how to use these indicators during the three-day Rule One virtual workshop.

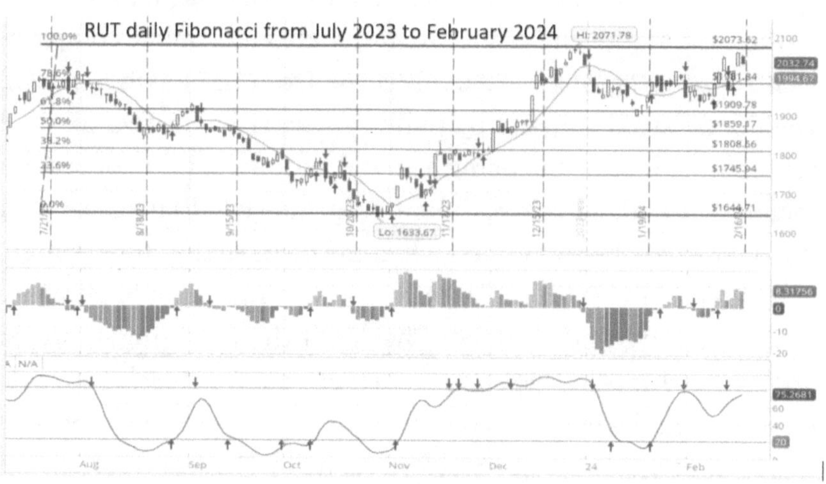

Three points to remember: 1. The more often the stock price bounces off the Floor or Ceiling, the stronger the Floor or

Ceiling becomes. 2. To determine how far the price will climb from the new Floor to reach the next Ceiling, look at the distance between the last Floor and the last Ceiling. 3. A price move of more than 3% above the Ceiling or below the Floor, accompanied by 150% of the average daily volume of shares traded, is a significant sign of a breakout that will last.

Floors and Ceilings (FACs) are predictable patterns in the price charts that show you the appropriate time to buy and sell. You can stockpile any time the price is below the MOS/Payback Time price, but buying on the FACs will help you buy at the best possible price. To maximize your long-term investment returns, buy near the Floor price. Be patient!

UNDERSTANDING DIVIDENDS

In today's investment landscape, there is a growing interest in acquiring stocks that offer dividends. It's appealing to possess ownership in a business and receive regular payments, akin to holding a treasury bill. Some individuals even consider dividends as the primary incentive for owning shares in a public company, as it represents tangible cash returns from the business itself. Dividends are disbursed by public enterprises for two distinct reasons, with only one being a sound rationale. I do not recommend the dividend reinvestment program (DRIP) because your dividends may be reinvested when the price of the stock is high. Use the cash dividends to live on, for option trading, or to purchase stocks that are undervalued. Check out the following dividend books: *The How To Book on Dividend Growth Investing: Create Generational Wealth and Passive Income for Life!* and *The Secrets to Maximizing Dividend Stock Returns* by Dr. Ace Goerig

The favorable reason is when a business accumulates more cash than it requires. A prudent CEO recognizes that this surplus belongs to the shareholders. The only justification for retaining it is if the CEO can utilize the funds to expand the business at a rate that justifies retaining the money. This growth rate is commonly known as Return on Equity (ROE), a critical metric. An effective CEO evaluates his team's performance, in part, based on how well they deploy owner capital. Indeed, overseeing the allocation of owner capital is arguably the CEO's most crucial responsibility. Returning the excess capital to shareholders becomes a legitimate option when the CEO cannot identify better investment opportunities.

The second reason is less commendable: some businesses allocate a portion of their earnings as a dividend to create the illusion of stability. This practice is influenced by Mr. Market, who prefers the appearance of steadiness over genuine stability. If earnings fluctuate, so does the dividend amount, causing unease for Mr. Market. He prefers a consistent dividend, resembling cash flow from a bond, and if this is achieved, he assigns a higher value to it. CEOs, responding to Mr. Market's preference, may establish an unwavering dividend quarter after quarter. This reliability attracts investors, especially retirees, who mistakenly associate a consistent dividend with a stable business and, therefore, low risk. These investors will not want to sell the stock even if it's going down because this will cause them to miss out on their quarterly dividend payments.

Dividends make sense when a business has no superior alternatives for deploying your funds. For retirees relying on dividend income for their living expenses, investing in a robust business with consistent dividends is prudent, if these dividends stem from genuine, free cash flow. To ascertain whether dividends are derived from sources other than cash flow, a crucial step is to examine the Cash Flow Statement of the business.

When you're trying to select the best dividend companies to buy, many experts recommend that you focus on those companies that have continually increased their dividends every year for a long period of time. These are called "dividend aristocrats," and "champions" that have increased their dividends every year for over 25 years. Those companies that have increased their dividends for more than 50 years are called dividend kings.

This is a starting point, but the most important focus in any investment is to buy those companies that give the highest total equity return over time. I focus more on companies that have high annual dividend growth and beat the S&P 500 over the last 10 years. Only 11 of the 56 dividend kings and 29 of the 90 dividend aristocrats and champions have done this.

To better understand why, let's compare two dividend kings. Lowe's (LOW) has increased their dividends for 63 years with a dividend yield of 2.08%. Northwest Natural (NWN) has increased their dividends for the past 66 years and has a dividend yield of 5.12%. If you chose Northwest Natural because of the high dividend yield, you would be making a big mistake. The focus must always be on the dividend growth and overall equity growth of the company.

Over the past 14 years, Lowe's, with a dividend yield of only 2.08%, had its share price grow from $28 a share to $221 (789% increase) in equity value. During the same time frame, Northwest Natural, with a dividend yield of 5.12%, had its **share price decrease,** from $44 per share to only $37.42 per share (15% decrease). Next let's look at annual dividend income. Lowe's (LOW) 100 shares of annual dividend income grew from $40 to $460 (1150% increase) compared to your 100 shares with Northwest Natural (NWN), where your dividend income only grew from $174 to $195 (11% increase).

I would rather own Lowe's that pays only a 2.08% dividend with an average 10-year annual dividend-growth rate of 19.8%, compared to NWN, that has a 5.12% dividend with an average 10-year dividend-growth rate of only 0.6%. Also, the Lowe's shares you bought 20 years ago are now paying a dividend return of 17% annually based on their original cost basis.

In 1988 Warren Buffett bought 23 million shares of Coca-Cola at a price of $2.73. With today's annual dividend rate of $1.94 per share, he gets an annual dividend return of 71% on the original shares bought. This year he will receive $776 million in dividends from Coca-Cola. Berkshire Hathaway does not pay dividends because Buffett feels he can better allocate the money for his investors. He still appreciates the power of dividend income and in 2024 will earn $6 billion in dividends from his investments.

This demonstrates the importance of focusing our purchases on companies with both high total equity-growth and high dividend-growth rate. This leads to ever-increasing personal dividend income over time. In strong dividend-growth companies, the dividends income you receive continues to grow each year, even if the price of the stock drops. Over time, the price of these wonderful companies will rebound as your dividend income increases every year. Warren Buffett said, "Time is the friend of a wonderful company and the enemy of the mediocre."

Many wonderful companies increase their dividends each year. This increased income gives comfort to those who live off their dividends, especially during negative times in the market. Texas Instruments (TXN) is an example of a wonderful company that demonstrates both incredible dividend growth and equity growth. In 2024, Texas Instruments was paying a dividend-income return of 34.7% on the original-cost-basis shares bought in 2009. Over the past 14 years, their dividends have grown from $45 per 100 shares to $520 in 2024. This is an 11.5 times increase in the dividends received over those years. In addition, a $100,000 investment in Texas Instruments in 2009 would have grown to more than $1.33 million in 2024.

Many retirees live on their dividends and unknowingly try to buy companies that have a high dividend yield without realizing that, over time, the value of their investment is continually decreasing. Do not be fooled by high dividend yields, as many companies will increase their dividend yield each year to lull shareholders into a false sense of security. This is why novice investors continue to hold the stock even as it continues to drop in value, or the company goes bankrupt.

General Motors (GM) consistently paid dividends for many years even though they borrowed money to do so. In 2009, during the financial crisis, they filed for bankruptcy; all common stock of the old GM Corporation became worthless, and investors lost all their money.

Always evaluate the strength and growth of the company before you buy. Once you own a company, check on the vital statistics of that company monthly. Sell these companies when the key indicators such as return on investment capital (ROIC) decrease, making the company no longer wonderful. Stay away from any company that has a payout ratio above 60%. The 5- and 10-year annual growth of the company needs to be better than the S&P 500 as a guideline before you buy any dividend-paying companies.

To determine the stock's annual equity yield, including reinvestments of dividends, go to https://dqydj.com/stock-return-calculator/. To determine equity growth, dividend growth and dividend yield, go to: https://seekingalpha.com/.

The dividend yield is a stock's annual dividend payment as a percentage of the stock price per share. Most dividend investors look for a yield somewhere between 2.5% and 6%. But the best total overall return comes from companies that have a lower than 2.5% dividend yield. Over time, you will be getting a higher dividend return in these high dividend-growth companies. In the example below, United Health (UNH) has a 1.48% dividend today. But the shares you bought 10 years before are now paying a dividend return of 10.2%, based on the price of the stock then. The shares of United Health (UNH) that you bought 20 years ago are paying you 23.8% today, based on your original share price. As they increased their yearly dividend, this return usually gets better and better over time.

You will notice in the chart below that the stock total return and dividend reinvestment came from those companies with lower dividend yields but had the highest 10-year average dividend-growth rates. Compare these companies with those on the bottom that have high dividend-yield and low dividend-growth rates. The average annual return, including dividend reinvestment on these high-dividend-yield companies (IBM, WBA, KO and JNJ), is significantly lower than the lower-dividend-yield companies over the past 10 years.

Let's now look at Broadcom, ticker symbol AVGO. Its dividend yield was only 1.68%, but it had a 10-year average dividend-growth rate of 39% and a whopping annual 10-year return of 39.5%. Over the past 10 years, a one-time **initial $10,000 investment grew to more than $272,000.** Compare this to Walgreen Boots Alliance (WBA), which had a 9.09% yield, and your initial investment of $10,000 declined to only $2,000 during that 10-year time frame, with dividends automatically reinvested. Over the same 10 years, $10,000 placed in the S&P 500 grew 3 times to $31,000.

It is important to keep high-returning companies on your watch list and take advantage of them when they become undervalued. You must wait for an event, such as we saw in March 2020, when the S&P 500 dropped 37%. This was a great time to buy these companies. Another event occurred in March 2009. Many great companies, such as Texas Instruments (TXN) and United Health (UNH), saw prices drop more than half. Texas Instruments dropped to $14 a share but grew to more than $200 a share by 2024. United Health Group went from $16 a share in 2009 to $591 a share by 2024. **Remember, "past performance is no guarantee of future results"!**

You will also note that most of the selected dividend-growth companies in the chart have a higher average annual return than the S&P 500 or even Warren Buffett's Berkshire Hathaway company.

Dividend Example: 2 January 2025

Ticker Symbol	Company	Sector	Cur Price	2025 Dividend	Dividend Yield	10Y ADGR	Cost basis Dividend yield in 10 years	Cost basis Dividend yield in 20 years	Annual total % return 2015 to 2025	$10k Return 2015 to 2025	SA 10 yr Total Return	P/E <20	Rule 1 Safety score
AVGO	Broadcom	IT	231	$2.36	1.02%	39.0%	9.7%	131.0%	37.2%	317	2882%	37	79
MSFT	Microsoft	IT	416	$3.32	0.80%	12.7%	8.1%	13.0%	27.3%	111	809%	32	99
AAPL	Apple Inc	IT	243	$1.00	0.41%	25.0%	5.0%	192.0%	26.7%	106	793%	35	82
COST	Costco	CS	904	$4.64	0.51%	12.8%	4.0%	15.5%	23.6%	82	582%	50	88
WSM	Williams Sonoma	CD	186	$2.28	1.23%	14.0%	7.8%	14.6%	19.9%	61	347%	18	93
UNH	United Health	HC	504	$8.40	1.67%	25.6%	10.2%	23.5%	19.2%	57	573%	21	88
TXN	Texas Instruments	IT	185	$5.44	2.94%	22.4%	11.0%	21.0%	17.0%	48	317%	38	55
HD	Home Depot	CD	387	$9.00	2.33%	20.3%	11.2%	25.0%	17.0%	48	337%	28	74
LOW	Lowe's	CD	246	$4.60	1.87%	18.9%	8.8%	17.0%	16.2%	44	329%	24	52
SHW	Sherwin-Williams	M	331	$2.86	0.86%	14.4%	4.8%	22.0%	15.4%	42	409%	34	64
BRK B	Berkshire Hathaway	ETF	450	$0.00	0.00%	NA	NA	NA	11.9%	31	233%	23	66
SPY	SPDR S&P500 ETF	ETF	581	$7.07	1.22%	7.4%	3.7%	6.0%	12.0%	31	198%	NA	NA
IBM	IBM	IT	220	$6.68	3.04%	5.1%	3.9%	7.9%	9.0%	23	38%	22	27
KO	Coca-Cola	CS	62	$1.94	3.13%	5.0%	4.9%	7.8%	7.2%	20	45%	22	53
JNJ	Johnson & Johnson	HC	144	$4.96	3.44%	6.0%	5.0%	9.0%	6.6%	19	38%	15	65
WBA	Walgreen Boots	CS	9.25	$1.00	10.81%	1.5%	1.5%	3.0%	-15.0%	2	-85%	6	14

Chart categories:

Sectors: information technology, healthcare, consumer staples, materials, consumer discretionary, exchange traded funds.

Cur Price: this is the current stock price.

Dividend: annual dollar dividend per share per year.

Dividend Yield: the current annual yield as a percentage (dividend/price x 100).

10Y AGDR is the average annual dividend-growth rate over the past 10 years. Dividend growth is the 2nd most important number in successful dividend investing over time. https://seekingalpha.com/symbol/AVGO/dividends/dividend-growth

Cost basis dividend yield in 10 years: the current annual yield as a percentage (current dividend/2014 price=? x 100 = %). (Example: in 2014 the price of Home Depot was $80, and the current annual dividend in 2025 is $9. You divide $9/$80 = .112 X 100 = 11.2% cost basis; you are now getting an 11.2% return today based on the price of the shares you bought 10 years before.

Cost-basis-dividend yield in 20 years: the current annual yield as a percentage (current dividend/2004 price=? x 100 = %). (Example: in 2004 the price of Home Depot was $36, and the current annual dividend in 2025 is $9. You divide $9/$36 = .25 X 100 = 25% cost basis). You are getting a 25% return today based on the price of the shares you bought 20 years before.

$10-K Stock Total Return 2015 to 2025: the total return in dollars with a $10,000 initial investment after 10 years. This is the most important number in successful dividend investing over time. With AVGO, a $10,000 investment in 2015 would have grown to $317,000 in those 10 years. In 2015, a $10,000 investment with IBM would have grown to only $22,000 by 2025 in those 10 years. Stock Total Return and Dividend Reinvestment (DRIP) average for 10 years from January 2015 to January 2025. https://dqydj.com/stock-return-calculator/

SA 10-year Return: the total return on the stock after 10 years using the Seeking Alpha website.

PE<20: this is the price-to-earnings ratio (price/earnings). Ideally, we would like to see it below 20.

Rule One safety score: this comes from the Rule One toolbox, which rates all stocks. The highest obtainable rating of 100 indicates a very strong and safe company, such as Microsoft, with a rating of 99, compared to a poor rating of 27 with IBM. The Rule One toolbox is a must for anyone who is involved in trading stocks. https://www.ruleonetoolbox.com/login

Data found on January 2025—https://seekingalpha.com/ https://dqydj.com/stock-return-calculator/ and https://www.ruleonetoolbox.com/ Below are examples using these websites for the chart on page 154.

Seekingalpha.com charting is one of the best ways to compare any stock to the S&P 500. Check your portfolio stocks and funds in Seeking Alpha to see how well you are doing. Below are examples of the 5-year and 10-year total returns of companies on the chart on page 154.

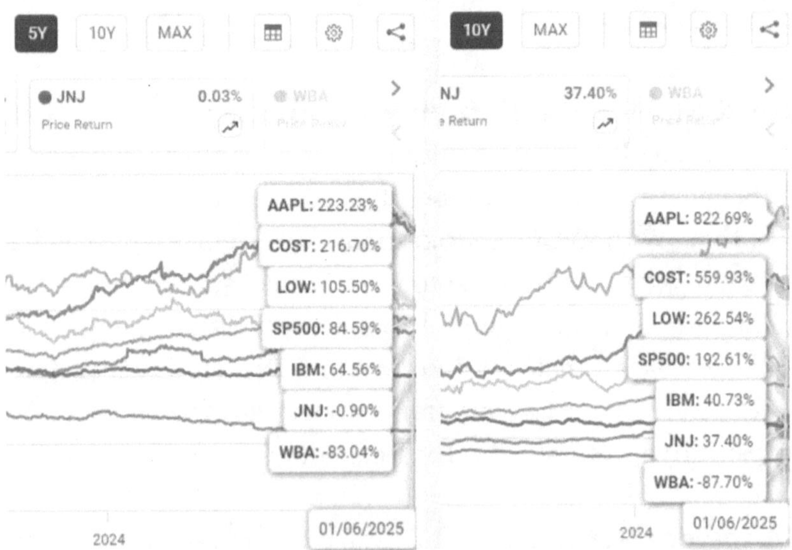

Use the stock-return calculator to determine the total stock return over a certain period of time (See below). https://dqydj.com/stock-return-calculator/ is

used to determine the Stock Total Return between 2015 and 2025 in dollars with a $10,000 initial investment after 10 years. Here we compare Costco (COST) with Walgreen Boots Alliance (WBA)

Use the Rule One toolbox to quickly evaluate the strength of companies (see below). https://www.ruleonetoolbox.com/ Costco (COST) has a moat score of 85 and a management score of 90, equaling and overall, **Rule One score of 88** out of 100. **Walgreens Boots (WBA)** has a moat score of 13 and a management score of 15, equaling and overall, **Rule One score of 14** out of 100.

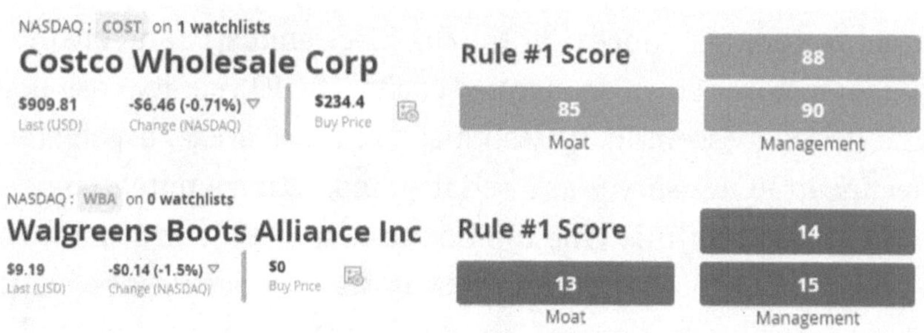

WHEN TO SELL

Warren Buffett once remarked, "The best time to sell a wonderful business is never." This is because he owns part of or the entire company and retains control over its cash flow. As small investors, we, too, would like to buy great companies on sale and keep them forever. But when the story changes and the company is no longer wonderful, we do have the advantage of getting out of the market in seconds, not like Warren Buffett or other institutional investors, who take 6 to 12 weeks to sell or buy into a company.

There are three scenarios when we might want to sell our stocks.

The first one is when we need the money. Planning for the future is crucial, ensuring that, when the day comes to sell, you have a range of options without significantly impacting your overall net worth. Anticipating this need allows you to select the businesses with the highest prices relative to their value, preventing forced sales during market downturns. Many retirees utilize their dividends to live on, but those who do not receive dividend income need to sell some of their stocks to live on.

The second reason to sell is when the fundamentals of a once-wonderful company have changed, and it is no longer a wonderful company. Industries and businesses can evolve, losing their appeal due to technological advancements or other factors. Vigilance over the Big Five—industry and business fundamentals, return on invested capital (ROIC), equity, cash flow, and debt—is essential. Any slippage in these areas, especially a decline in ROIC, serves as a red flag, indicating a potential need to exit. Use the Rule One toolbox to help you determine these numbers. Warren Buffett reminds us that, if a business no longer aligns with your understanding or violates fundamental principles, it may be time to exit. Don't wait to hope the price will go back up—sell, and take the loss.

The third time we would sell is when the market price significantly exceeds the Sticker Price (retail value). While the initial approach involves buying at a low price, selling occurs when the price surpasses the Sticker Price (companies' intrinsic value price) by 20%. This strategy takes advantage of market euphoria, allowing you to potentially repurchase the business at a discount within a year or two, as Mr. Market's exuberance tends to be short-lived.

The decision to sell when the price is 20% above intrinsic value is based on growth rate. If the company has a strong growth rate, such as 15% a year or greater, it may be wise just to hold the company and not sell. But if the company is growing at only 4%, then selling the company may be a good idea. Phil Town has said some of the biggest errors he has made is getting out of great companies too early.

Three of the greatest investors of all time, Warren Buffett, Jack Bogle and Peter Lynch, believe that, as long as the company continues to be wonderful, you never sell. You must be prepared financially and psychologically to hold them through thick and thin.

WHERE TO PUT YOUR MONEY NOW

As of November 2024, the market is at its all-time high, and we have yet to have an event where we can buy great companies at half price. In order of preference, here are some suggestions.

Finish paying off debt, which will always give you the highest guaranteed return while you learn to paper trade in the market through *thinkorswim.*

Schwab money-market account (SWVXX) is a good interim place for your money while you are waiting to get into the market. As of this writing, their annual return is about 5%. These are not FDIC insured, but they are SIPC insured up to $500,000. This fund is available for individual retirement and investment accounts. If your account is a corporation, a trust, or 401(k), then you would use either the Schwab Government Money

Fund (SWVXX) or the Schwab Treasury Obligations Money Fund (SNOXX), also returning about 5% today, January 2025.

Warren Buffett doesn't like holding large amounts of cash and would rather be investing that money and using it to generate strong returns, however, he also refuses to buy stocks unless prices are attractive. Today, he believes the stock market is extremely overvalued, and now Berkshire Hathaway has a record $277 billion in cash. He is very happy to earn 5% on that money while he waits for stocks to go on sale.

Option trading: the goal in Rule One investing is to buy 6 to 15 wonderful companies at the right price. This may take some time when the market is at its all-time high, like it is today. Option trades are done over a 5-day to a 30-day period, allowing your money to be available for those events where you can buy your wonderful company at half price. To make money while you wait, you may want to learn to do option trading correctly. You need to have a good system; this is best reviewed and discussed in the three-day virtual Zoom Rule One course.

Many option traders lose money because they have no system. In the Rule One Zoom course, you will learn specific rules to use for trading options that have been shown to have a 95% success rate, with an annual return of 15% to 30% a year. If done right, option trading can replace your income. As you practice paper trading, you will gain high confidence in the Rule One approach to option trading. **Once they have learned the Rule One approach to option trading correctly, many Rule One investors quit their day job and make a higher income with option trading. This can be a lifesaver for retirees who have not saved well for retirement.**

These trades are done with wonderful companies that you want to own anyway. Rule One also offers a two-year advanced course with excellent instructors for those who want to expand their investing knowledge and learn more about step-by-step option trading. Here you can practice with paper money in your simulated *thinkorswim* trading account with no risk. In 2023, the Rule One study group did more than 120 real option trades with only one loss (99% success) and an annual return of more than 42%. It was a very good year.

Buy wonderful companies at half price. We must wait for an event to occur that pushes the stock to a half-price Margin of Safety level. This can happen when there is a company or market event and during volatile times, such as during a long bear market. Remember what Charlie Munger said: **"You make money in the stock market not when you buy or not when you sell but when you wait."**

SHOULD YOU INVEST IN STOCKS OR IN REAL ESTATE?

You need to select the area of investment which you feel best suited for and understand in depth. Traditional real-estate investments can be broken down into two broad categories: residential properties—like your home, rental properties or flipping homes to buy and then resell for a profit—and commercial properties, such as apartment complexes, office buildings and strip malls.

Personally, I am not a big fan of real estate for many reasons. Here are some of those reasons. https://www.nerdwallet.com/article/investing/real-estate-vs-stocks-which-is-the-better-investment

Real-estate investments can be more work than stocks. While purchasing property is easy to understand, that doesn't mean the work of maintaining properties, especially rental properties, is easy. Owning properties requires much more sweat equity than purchasing stock or stock investments like mutual funds.

Real estate is expensive and highly illiquid. Investing in real estate, even when borrowing cash, requires a large upfront investment. Getting your money out of a real-estate investment through resale is much more difficult than the point-and-click ease of buying and selling stocks.

Real estate has high transaction costs. A seller can expect to pay significant closing costs, which can take as much as 6% to 10% off the top of the sale price. That's a hefty cut compared with stocks, especially now that most brokers charge no fees for stock trades.

It's difficult to diversify your investments with real estate. Location matters when investing in real estate. Sales may slump in one area, while values explode in another. Diversifying the purchase of real-estate properties by location and type (a mix of residential and commercial, for example) requires much deeper pockets than the average investor has.

The return on your investment isn't a sure thing. While property prices tend to rise over time, there's always a risk of selling a property at a loss—the 2008 financial crisis and post-pandemic uncertainty in the housing market are reminders of that. This is also true of stocks, of course.

THE PROs OF INVESTING IN STOCKS

Over time, investments in stocks have done much better than real estate. The US median home price in 1973 was $33,500, and, by today's standards, it has increased to $431,000. This growth represents an average annual return of 5.24%. In comparison, if you had invested that same $33,500 into the S&P 500 in 1973, your investment would now be worth a staggering $5.1 million, translating to an annual return of 10.59%.

Stocks are highly liquid. While investment cash can be locked up for years in real estate, the purchase or sale of public-company shares can be done the moment you decide it's time to act. Unlike real estate, it's also easier to know the value of your investment at any time.

It's easier to diversify your investment in stocks. Few people have the time—let alone the cash—to purchase enough real-estate properties to cover a broad enough range of locations or industries to have true diversification. With stocks, it's possible to build a broad portfolio of companies and industries at a fraction of the time and cost of owning a diverse collection of properties. The easiest way to get that diversification is to purchase shares in mutual funds, index funds or exchange-traded funds. These funds buy shares in a wide swath of companies, which can give fund investors instant diversification.

There are fewer (if any) transaction fees with stocks. While you'll need to open a brokerage account to buy and sell stocks, the price war among discount brokers has reduced stock-trading costs to $0 in most cases. Many brokers also offer a selection of non-transaction-fee mutual funds, index funds and ETFs.

You can grow your investment in tax-advantaged retirement accounts. Purchasing shares through an employer-sponsored retirement account like a 401(k) or through an individual retirement account can allow your investment to grow tax-deferred or even tax-free.

THE CONs OF STOCK INVESTING

Stock prices are much more volatile than real estate. The prices of stocks can move up and down much faster than real-estate prices. That volatility can be stomach-churning unless you take a long view on the stocks and funds you purchase for your portfolio, meaning you plan to buy and hold despite volatility.

Selling stocks may result in a capital-gains tax. When you sell your stocks, you may have to pay a capital-gains tax. If you've held the stock for more than a year, however, you may qualify for taxes at a lower rate. Also, you may have to pay taxes on any stock dividends your portfolio paid out during the year. (Understand more about taxes on stocks.)

Stocks can trigger emotional decision-making. While you can buy and sell stocks more easily than real-estate properties, that doesn't mean you should. When markets waver, investors often sell when a buy-and-hold strategy typically produces greater returns. Investors should take a long view of all investments, including building a stock portfolio.

Praise for

The Dentist Guide to Creating Personal and Financial Freedom

Dr. Ace Goerig is a genius when it comes to unlocking the keys to finances and happiness in life! He loves sharing his easy-to-implement secrets of contentment, enthusiasm, and living the good life . . . all at the same time. He has studied burned-out employers/employees in the workforce for decades. From the CEO/owner to the entry-level employees, workers are simply tired of the noose around their necks called "debt."

We all know that debt reduction at a fast pace is the key to this thirst for "working because we love it" versus hating for Monday to roll around to go back to the paycheck-to-paycheck existence. Ace's book outlines exactly what others can do to achieve this ravenous happiness in life. There are several key elements: Live below your means early on; pay yourself first each payday; be the most ethical person you know; hire experts to provide the growth in your business that compounds your net by tens of thousands per month. This not only pays down the debt quickly—it also allows you to work because you "get to" rather than "have to." That, folks, is pure happiness.

—**Linda Miles, Founder/CEO**, Linda Miles & Associates
Founder, Speaking Consulting Network

Ace has created a blueprint that has been found tried and true thousands of times. You are fortunate that you don't have to reinvent the wheel or spend one more day struggling only to find another strategy that does not work. This is a playbook for success in life in which Ace outlines a concise, consistent financial plan for dentists that works.

—**Michael Abernathy, DDS**
Founder of Summit Practice Solutions

A superb book! Dr. Goerig demonstrates the keys to happiness and financial success. The core of his message is to become financially free while enjoying your life. Money in and of itself will not make you happy, but having enough money not to have to worry about money allows you to develop your passions. Build enough wealth through conservative, proven investments, get out of debt, gain perspective, and then use most of your time cultivating a life that is real, a life based on what you want, not what your parents or society tells you to be. Follow his advice, all of it, and I assure you that you will be 1,000% better for it!

—**Alex Nottingham, JD, MBA**
Founder & CEO of All-Star Dental Academy

Every dentist should keep this book bedside and read and re-read it. The advice is sound and easy to understand and implement. I consider Ace Goerig as a combination of John Bogle and Warren Buffett for dentists who want a secure financial future.

—**Dan Solin**
Author of the Smartest series of investing books

I've known Ace for 35 years, and he has always been focused on value, quality, self-improvement and mentoring others. This book is a continuation of those attributes and gives the reader the skills and knowledge to live a life of peace, joy, hope, contentment, achievement and financial freedom. By putting his principles into action, you will be able to claim "victory," and that success will spread to your office team, your patients and, most importantly, your family.

—**James C. Kulild, DDS, MS**, Past President,
American Association of Endodontists, Diplomate,
American Board of Endodontics, Professor Emeritus,
Department of Endodontics UMKC School of Dentistry

As a dentist in practice for 15 years, I have often struggled with who to believe when it came to investing and a financial philosophy for life. I often was torn between what was the best way to live, spend, and save. It is such an important topic, with so many different opinions on the "right way." I found Ace 5 years ago, and he and his philosophy have totally changed my life. All my questions were answered, and all the secrets are contained in this short book. I truly believe that this is the "right" way and have made a commitment to read this book at the beginning of each year to remind myself. Thank you, Ace. I am now living a more meaningful, happy, purposeful, almost-debt-free life because of you and your relentless passion to help others.

—**Derek White, DDS**
Madison, MS

This book is one of the most comprehensive and compelling publications on the subject that I have experienced. Its uniqueness and what differentiates it from others is that it specifically addresses the lifelong needs and goals of dentists everywhere—issues and subject matter certainly not taught in our nation's dental schools. This book is a terrific read for all of us at any stage of our career, to and through retirement.

—**Hugh Habas, DDS**
New Jersey national presenter on practice management

Here it is, in a wonderful, compact nutshell—the "crux" of the Ace Goerig philosophy of practice, personal finance and life boiled down to this beautiful guide for happiness in our practice and personal life! Why "recreate the wheel" when you have the best practice-management mentor generously sharing his experiences and wisdom with you for a life filled with peace, joy and fulfillment? This book is a must-read for all dentists, and it gives us life skills to share with our loved ones, too!

—**Richard C. Wittenauer, DDS**
Diplomate, ABE, California

www.ingramcontent.com/pod-product-compliance
Lightning Source LLC
LaVergne TN
LVHW090405210926
848480LV00002B/454

* 9 7 9 8 9 9 1 3 1 7 3 0 6 *